While it's tempting to gather up the hurts and regrets of the past and walk through life feeling disillusioned and sad, that's not truly living. And that's why we need a friend like Bianca. In her wise and relatable way, she speaks powerful truth while guiding us out of negative habits and debilitating tendencies. What's happened in the past doesn't get to dictate what's up ahead when we have Jesus. If you want to look forward to an exciting future, this book is a must-read!

Lysa TerKeurst, #1 *New York Times* bestselling author
and president of Proverbs 31 Ministries

Bianca's book is like the coolest and realest big sister, speaking truth to our generation! Her practical, helpful, and hilarious life tips will help readers become the best version of themselves—the selves God intended them to be.

Sadie Robertson, author, speaker & founder of Live Original

Bianca has been a friend of mine for a long time. She loves God and expresses that love in practical ways. This book is chock-full of ideas to help you navigate your life with faith, resilience, and joy.

Bob Goff, Chief Balloon Inflator and author of *Love Does*

How to Have Your Life Not Suck is one of those books that will empower the next generation. Layered with biblical truth and modern-day examples, Bianca dives deep into the heart and provides practical handles for dealing with life. Funny and relevant, her words will help many and serve as a reminder that we all need some tips and tools to have our lives not suck.

Lisa Bevere, *New York Times* bestselling author
and cofounder of Messenger International

No one wants to have a bad day or be in a foul mood, but we ofter allow our thinking and behavior to lead us back to these well roads with a kind of spiritual amnesia. Your life doesn' Groundhog's Day over and over again; you can if you want to, and Bianca will show you h

Levi Lusko, pa
Through the E   *War*

With clarity, humor, and practical application, Bianca gently encourages the next generation to grow up well. I can't wait to see how this book helps people mature and step into all God has called them to.

Jasmine Star, world-renowned photographer, entrepreneur, and digital influencer

Energizing. Hilarious. Helpful. Bianca Olthoff is the best friend we all long for, the one who will walk us through the treacherous territory of adulthood. *How to Have Your Life Not Suck* is jam-packed with wisdom and wit to help guide us through life, love, and everything in between. Grab a girlfriend and put this book at the top of your reading list today.

Shelley Giglio

Bianca Oltoff is consistently encouraging but won't let you get away with anything. This book is that kind of friend, too. She has put on these pages what she would say to you over a coffee or from the treadmill next to you or in a voice memo that you play before you walk into a big meeting. I'm sure you're going to love this book because it's what being friends with Bianca is really like: the best.

Annie F. Downs, bestselling author of *100 Days to Brave* and host of the *That Sounds Fun* podcast

HOW TO HAVE YOUR LIFE NOT SUCK

BIANCA JUÁREZ OLTHOFF

ZONDERVAN

How to Have Your Life Not Suck
Copyright © 2019 by Bianca Juárez Olthoff

Requests for information should be addressed to:
Zondervan, *3900 Sparks Dr. SE, Grand Rapids, Michigan 49546*

ISBN 978-0-310-34526-8 (softcover)

ISBN 978-0-310-35592-2 (audio)

ISBN 978-0-310-34527-5 (ebook)

The author is represented by the literary agency of Alive Communications, Inc., 8585 Criterion Drive, Unit 63060, Colorado Springs, Colorado 80920-1045, www.alivecommunications.com.

Cover design: Micah Kandros
Cover photography: Meshali Mitchell

Printed in the United States of America

19 20 21 22 23 LSC 10 9 8 7 6 5 4 3 2

To Zoe Belle, Ryen Blake, and Chelsie Marlene:

I may not have made you in my womb, but
I've loved you with all my heart. This book
is for the generation of women you will raise.
I hope you take these words to heart, make
them your own, and share them with others.

~B

CONTENTS

=

Part 3: Adulting and Growing Up

FOREWORD

"Do you want to change the world?"

I will never forget the day I asked Bianca Olthoff this question. We were eating hummus and pita bread, while talking a million miles an hour—loudly. I guess that's what happens when you put a Greek woman and a Puerto Rican woman at the same table. It was her passion and humor that caught my attention, and her audacity and compassion that kept it. I could tell this was a young woman who wanted to love the world like Jesus and live an extraordinary life for his glory. She wasn't normal. I loved that about her. I still do.

"Of course I want to change the world," she said.

There was a long pause, and then I challenged her to commit to a season of coaching and training that would help her to become who she needed to be, to do what she had been called to do. It would not be easy, and it was not for the fainthearted. At that point in her life, she did not need a cheerleader to encourage her, but a coach to really push her. She was obviously an extraordinarily gifted young woman, full of potential, but in order to realize that potential, she would need to commit to the process of growth and transformation.

Few are willing to embark upon that painful path.

The way is narrow.

To live a life of service to others, you must learn to die to self.

Crucifying the flesh is never easy.

Always messy.

She looked at me, and I saw her think long and hard about what her future would look like. She took a deep breath and said yes. Thus began our adventure working alongside one another, fighting to abolish slavery everywhere forever through The A21 Campaign.

Bianca has fought hard to ensure that her own life does not suck and shares her wisdom with us as only she can. Full of truth and humor, she takes God's Word and makes it applicable to our everyday lives. If the Bible is the guide, Bianca has translated the guide to reach the next generation.

Using the story of Ruth—an Old Testament heroine with a pockmarked past—Bianca makes some of life's difficult topics like suffering, growing up, heartbreak, and friendship not only survivable, but relatable.

I've been a firsthand witness to seeing Bianca walk roads that have made her stronger and wiser. I love her with all my heart. I know you will too.

Christine Caine,
founder of A21 and Propel Women
and author of *Unashamed*,
Undaunted, and *Unexpected*

THE BEGINNING

―――

"I just wish someone would've told me this *years* ago," Ashley groaned, covering her face with her hands.

We sat at a small table near the coffee shop window, sipping drinks and eating lunch. Like lightning, her words struck me, momentarily illuminating my thoughts. My wish was the same—that someone would've told me what I was telling her when I was her age.

I've never considered myself to be a guru, coach, or mentor because those roles seem reserved for Dr. Phil, therapists, and sage pastors. But one thing I did know: I was good at reading the Bible and talking about Jesus. And that was how Ashley and I connected.

One Sunday morning I stood behind a podium and taught about one of the greatest stories in history, one that has captured my heart. It's a story of trial and triumph, pain and promise, a story of two women from two different generations, two different backgrounds, and two different countries who came together and witnessed the invisible hand of God moving in their lives. One of the women had weathered life's greatest losses, suffered a crisis of faith, and felt old and washed up, without a future or hope. The other woman had her entire life before her but had nothing to rely on, build upon, or inherit. They supported each other in their journey to find home, family, community, and purpose.

This rags-to-riches story of redemption is the stuff that

makes film writers swoon. And it's all recounted in a small Old Testament book named after the heroine, Ruth.

My deep love for the story of Ruth permeated my words as I preached that Sunday morning. Ashley—who sat alone in the full sanctuary—hung on every word. After the church service, she found me in the courtyard and asked me one question, which morphed into a conversation and eventually led to us sipping drinks over lunch in Orange County, California.

My new friend was twenty-seven years old, a college graduate living with roommates in an apartment they could barely afford. She was attractive and smart and outgoing—and as single as a Pringle ready to mingle. Recovering from a string of bad relationships, and having watched her parents' marriage implode during her high school years, she found herself in church in search of ~~meaning purpose a relationship~~ . . . well, she really didn't know. But she knew her life sucked, and she needed *something*.

After months of roaming the church campus and connecting with no one her age, Ashley's attendance at church and interest in spiritual things was waning as her brunch-and-workout routine momentarily satiated her desire for community and meaning.

Ashley had so much potential, so many opportunities, so many roads before her, but she suffered from what I diagnosed as Analysis Paralysis. I know I'm not a psychologist, but I've coined my own "diagnosis" for women who struggle to find the right partner, fight loneliness, and/or can't move forward when they're feeling stuck.

You might recognize these symptoms:

- Inability to make decisions
- Confusion and fear of the future
- An inordinate feeling of being left behind and not knowing how to move forward
- Staring at people with a frozen smile and wide, darting

eyes when they ask what you are going to do with your
life (because you know you couldn't even decide what
jeans to wear that morning)

On a random Sunday morning at church, as Ashley sat in a
sea of faces she didn't know, something struck her. It wasn't my
awesome biblical knowledge or exegesis. It wasn't even the killer
fake eyelashes I wore. Ashley was struck with the truth of God's
Word. Sure, I did my best to make the biblical text fun and relevant, but there is NOTHING like the power of God's Word coming
to life.

That morning, sitting in church alone, Ashley felt like God
was speaking to *her*.

"I mean, I know there were thousands of people in church
this morning, but God was speaking to me through Ruth's story,"
she explained awkwardly, as if I might laugh at her recollection
of the morning.

But I knew exactly what she was feeling. I'd had the same
experience.

<hr />

Ten years before, as a twenty-five-year-old living at home with my
parents, I was in graduate school, licking my wounds after a bad
breakup, and dealing with my mom's second round of cancer. Life
sucked. I wanted a therapist—or at least someone wise—to come
alongside me and tell me what to do with my life, tell me which
guys to stay away from, tell me which type of jeans would make
my thighs look thinner. But even more than that, what I wanted
was someone to look into my eyes and tell me, "No matter what
happens, life is going to be okay."

I never had a mentor or "life coach" (whatever that means), but
I always believed characters in the Bible were my actual friends.

As a child, I loved church and Sunday school and vacation Bible school and summer camp because they were chances to learn more about my Bible friends. If Deborah from Judges 4 were alive today, I would make it my mission to become her political staffer and learn how to lead like her. If Lazarus's sister Mary lived in California, I would invite her to lunch and ask her what inspired her to acts of love without fear of judgment. If Paul were still walking the earth, I would invite him to our church and ask him to teach us how to break down theology in an easy way like he did for the Colossians and Ephesians. Better yet, I'd ask him how he fought off loneliness and isolation while he was imprisoned for living out his calling.

(This list could go on and on because, in my mind, I have *lots* of friends from the Bible.)

But if I could pick one woman to be my BFF, it would be Ruth. Ruth was in the middle of a spiritual desert, having lost everything—her love, her financial security, her family, her dreams—and decided then and there, with confidence, who she was going to be in the midst of her loss. Without a map, a mentor, or a social media following, Ruth decided **where** she was going, **who** she was going to follow, and **how** she was going to live.

Though these amazing characters aren't alive today, I believe their stories can serve as modern-day playbooks for how to live, lead, and love.

In my own desert season at twenty-five, as I questioned my faith—when I lost my security, my dreams, and the man I believed I was going to marry—I became friends with these women on their desert journey back home to Bethlehem. Naomi was a wise old woman who taught Ruth (and me) to express grief but trust God, to have hope but work hard, to be guarded but vulnerable.

Through time, lessons learned, and strengthened faith, I have become wiser and taken ownership of the title *mentor*. You might not be Ruth. I might not be Naomi. But I can safely wager we both have gone through our fair share of desert seasons. We are two different women from two different backgrounds and possibly from two different generations, but I've learned some valuable lessons I want to share with you. Learn from my mistakes and glean from my experience.

———

That conversation with Ashley led to many more with other young women who echoed her sentiment: *How can we learn today what we need to know for tomorrow?* What I discovered through countless conversations and coffee dates is that when you are stuck and confused, you don't need finger wagging or nagging. You need a guide who can point you to your proverbial Bethlehem, who can remind you there is a God who provides, and who will look you in the eye and say, "No matter what happens, life is going to be okay."

No matter what happens, life is going to be okay.

I'm here to be your guide (minus the cargo shorts and tacky hat). I have made my share of mistakes, which have caused me heartache, but I've found my way back and want to help you avoid taking the same unnecessary detours. Adulting is hard and mistakes can cost you time and energy, resulting in loneliness and pain. In that vein, I want to share with *you* what I've learned about life from my friends Ruth and Naomi.

In Part 1 we will discuss relationships and how to date well. Part 2 explores some questions around faith and how to survive trials with our spirituality intact. Finally, in Part 3 we will have some hard chats about growing up and living toward our legacy.

And because I already love you so much, I've invited my dear friend Dr. Deborah Gorton, clinical psychologist and Dean of Psychology at Moody Bible Institute, to help us through some tough topics by sharing her wisdom and perspective. Look for her input in the sections called *Thoughts from a Therapist*. (This is basically free therapy, so you're welcome! You've already started making your life not suck, and you're doing it at a bargain rate.) I have known Dr. Deb for the last five years and have learned so much from her lectures, not to mention from her life. She is a therapist with a teacher's heart. The wisdom she has imparted to me has changed the way I think and has given me the ability to believe I can be all that I'm called to be.

If generations of women have gone before us and survived loss, fear, trauma, and stretch marks, so will we.

And sometimes that's all we need to get back up and keep walking.

Join me as we figure out how to make your life not suck.

STOP! READ THIS FIRST!

Before you read this book, you're going to need to know a little bit about the life and times of Ruth the Moabitess. If you've read the small book of Ruth in the pages of the Old Testament, you're already one leg up! But to make sure we are all on the same page, here is a Disney version of one of the greatest stories ever told.

Once upon a time, in a land far away, lived a woman who had lost everything. Ruth was born in a crazy city with a bad reputation, but in the midst of the chaos, she found a Jewish hunk by the name of Mahlon who married her and welcomed her into his holy Hebrew family. Sadly, tragedy struck, and before Ruth could have a baby, her father-in-law passed away. In another fatal family blow, her brother-in-law Kilion died before her sister-in-law, Orpah, could produce the next family heir. And if things seemed like they couldn't get any worse for this young woman with infertility issues, they did. In tragic form, she lost her husband to illness.

Three dead men left three living women with no home and no income in Moab, a land deemed unacceptable for good Jews because of its questionable history of incest and pagan worship. Naomi, Ruth's mother-in-law, therefore decided to return to her hometown of Bethlehem to try to find refuge among her people.

All three widows began the desert trek to Bethlehem. But on a hot, dusty road halfway between Moab and Bethlehem, the matriarch broke down. Having lost her husband and two sons—with no heir produced by either of her sons' widows—Naomi urged her two daughters-in-law to go back to their homeland. Orpah turned back to Moab accordingly, but Ruth refused to leave her mother-in-law, vowing to love Naomi, her people, and her God from then on.

Upon the women's arrival in Bethlehem, life didn't get easier. On the brink of starvation, Ruth decided to look for work in the fields—a job that would entail hard manual labor. She found herself in a field belonging to a landowner by the name of Boaz. Ruth was treated kindly and protected by this man of honor and was given food not only for herself, but for Naomi as well.

When Naomi found out that Ruth was working in Boaz's field, she became a true Jewish *yenta* and tried playing matchmaker. Encouraging her daughter-in-law to spruce herself up, Naomi instructed her beloved Ruth to let Boaz know she was single. In an unheard-of move for a Jewish love story, Ruth initiated a DTR, and Boaz responded immediately. Then Boaz married Ruth and welcomed her mother-in-law into the family. He was a great guy.

But the love story doesn't end there. In true fairy tale fashion, Ruth became pregnant and bore a son, whom Naomi loved as her own. The story of Ruth and Naomi proves to us that even when life feels hopeless, we can hope for a beautiful beginning to a new chapter.

PART 1

Dating and Relationships

Dating is one of the hardest relational minefields to navigate in adulthood, am I right? Because the church has remained largely silent about relationships other than marriages, we've turned over the narrative and allowed magazines, movies, and media to tell us what love, dating, and sex should look like in our culture. Leery of listening to the wrong voices, I became passionate about the topic of dating and relationships (and secretly hope to make #bHarmony a thing so I can become a matchmaker for all my single friends). I felt it necessary for us, as wise followers of Jesus, to take back the narrative of healthy dating relationships and learn from someone who braved the minefield—and survived to tell us about it.

Enter Ruth. She isn't a dating guru or a model for successful single living, but she leans upon the wisdom of an older woman and takes calculated risks in the process of getting to know someone. In this section, get ready to take tips from Dr. Deb, read about other women's dating experiences, and walk away with some wisdom from Ruth and Naomi, such as:

- The value of dating someone with a job (HELLO!)
- How to fearlessly communicate what you want
- The difference between being vain and being clean
- Accepting gifts doesn't mean you're a gold digger
- Why you should have high dating standards

Perhaps you are married and feel like this section no longer applies to you. Take heed, lest ye fall, my dear sister. The act of getting to know someone—*dating*—never ends, even after you say *I do*. But if you are beyond the conversation, you probably have single friends, coworkers, or family members who have questions about dating that perhaps you've lost the answers for. This section will refresh and remind you of ways you can support, love, and guide your single sisters.

CHAPTER 1

ACCEPTABLE STALKING

Boaz asked the overseer of his harvesters, "Who
does that young woman belong to?"
RUTH 2:5

"Do you think what we are doing is wrong? Isn't this intrusive?"
Marlee asked, genuinely concerned. I waved my hand in the air
as if swatting the annoying words away.

"Listen," I insisted, "we are doing *research*."

Marlee—a single and vivacious twenty-two-year-old—met a
guy at church who had commented on a few of her social media
posts and even direct messaged her. Unsure of his intentions, she
asked me what I thought.

Without thinking twice, I pulled out my phone and googled
his name. With the help of the World Wide Web, I found a host
of information about him and tracked down his social media
accounts. We huddled over my iPhone like FBI agents stalking
a terrorist—we needed all the information we could find. Why?
Because if there was going to be an advance into "foreign territory" (aka dating), she needed to be prepared.

Ten years ago, before the explosion of online dating and social media, *stalking* was a word reserved for weird men with scraggly hair and maybe a murky cockeye (à la your awkward next-door neighbor to whom you've never spoken a word). But with social media boasting four billion daily users, we have made internet "stalking" of potential boyfriends socially acceptable. Not only is it acceptable, it is a valuable tool when it comes to getting to know someone you're attracted to from a safe distance.

To ensure we aren't being driven by the lusts of the flesh (aka "eye candy"), let's take a clue from our friend Boaz.

In Ruth 2, we see Boaz enter the story. Business owner and bad@$$ boss, he visits his enterprise and scopes out the land. The employees are hard at work when the owner of the field surveys his holdings. As he is going over the daily routine, he catches sight of someone new working the fields.

What does he do?

Does he copy the swagger of his biblical ancestor Joshua, march down to the field, and whisper to Ruth, "Girl, are you Jericho? Because I will walk around you seven times if it will make you fall for me."

Negative. He doesn't. Instead of swooping in and making some smooth moves on the young Moabitess, Boaz observes her from afar.

We can learn a few things from the type of man Boaz was. For starters, he was intimately aware of who was in his field. A foreigner in his field caught his eye, and he did some research to find out who she was. Because Boaz didn't have the handy help of Facebook or Instagram, he relied on the tried-and-true form of acquiring the background of a new person: he asked a trusted colleague, his overseer.

"Who does that young woman belong to?"

In a culture where family was your identity, your land and lineage said everything anyone needed to know about you. (More on this in chapter 8.) Unfortunately, Ruth had two strikes against her. Not only was she an immigrant, she was an immigrant from a despised land, Moab. As people who were birthed out of incest and worshipers of a false god, Ruth's family would have been ostracized and despised among the chosen children of Israel.

If the conversation had stopped there, Ruth's story might have ended as quickly as it began. But the overseer revealed to Boaz that Ruth was a hard worker who didn't take lots of breaks. In that small byline, that brief inclusion, Ruth's character spoke louder than her social status, marital status, or immigration status. Thank goodness there is always more to our stories; our history and heritage do not determine our outcomes.

This is why I believe there is something wildly important about getting to know someone from a distance. When we become intimate with a person (through conversation, close proximity, and emotional connection), our judgment and decision-making can become clouded.

For example, I attended a small liberal arts college in California. The entire student body consisted of fewer than three thousand students, and only a thousand lived on campus. The dating scene was always interesting because returning students vowed they would never date _____ (fill in the blank). My friends and classmates would list a host of requirements and a litany of *nevers*. But after the first semester of late-night study sessions, college parties, and dorm life, everybody's nonnegotiable standards about what they were looking for in the opposite sex became a blur, a phenomenon commonly referred to as *wearing beer goggles*. As in, you drink until someone looks attractive.

The problem with dating or "going out" without investigating (especially when we're feeling limited, lonely, or, worse, inebriated) is that we make poor decisions, we lower our standards, and we think what's in front of us is all there will ever be.

Boaz waited and researched from afar. Thanks to social media and the internet, so can we.

If you are interested in someone, do your research! It's easy to become infatuated with someone up close, so do your investigating from a distance. Like the proverb warns us: *guard your heart and put down the beer goggles*. (Okay, fine. I added that last part, but Solomon would've agreed with me.)

Here are some tips on how to investigate someone online in the appropriate manner.

GOOGLE. Google is a search engine that can help you find the best place to eat in your area, trending news, and—lo and behold—it's also great for cyberstalking a potential date.

Just so we are clear, I'm a cyberstalker and proud of it. Not only have I stalked online every man I've ever dated, to this day I creep every conference and church I speak at. I visit their website, check out their social media, and even click on their hashtags. Why? Because the internet is the best way to find out not only what people say about themselves, but what *other people* say about them.

If I googled a guy and discovered he was voted Beer Kegger Champion of his college, was tagged in tons of photos half-dressed at parties, and every photo in Google Images was taken with a different girl, I'd probably think twice about going out with him.

And before anyone judges me and says, "But Bianca, we are NEW creations in Christ and God forgives us of all stupidity! Don't be so judgmental," let me say this: you're right. But if there's nothing online to balance out the half-dressed party animal pictures (deworming children in Somalia, serving his local homeless community, being—I don't know—*sober*), then that's a red flag.

On the other hand, if someone has no online presence at all, that's also a red flag. Like, have you been living in a hermit commune with no internet? Who are you, Ted Bundy?

Use this ~~gift from God~~ tool to learn more about the people you're thinking about doing life with.

SOCIAL MEDIA. I love social media. I consistently say social media is the greatest social equalizer. Prior to social media, we would never have had access to the president of the United States (unless you were, like, super cool and could pull strings in politics). But now, all I have to do is tag @POTUS, and I have directly communicated to the leader of the free world.

What we put out on social media is a reflection of who we are, what we believe, and who we engage with. (Note: I did not say social media *is* who we are. Social media is a *curated reflection* of who we are and how we want to be perceived. More on this from Dr. Deb later.)

You can learn so much about someone by ~~stalking~~ researching his social media accounts. Does he share your values? Does he like the same things you do? Can he spell? All this can be learned simply by scrolling through someone's social media profile.

Don't believe everything on the internet . . . maybe just half of it. Because it's likely at least half of it is true.

ASK FRIENDS. What Boaz did by asking his overseer about Ruth was even better than googling her, because the best way to get to know someone is to ask their friends. Nothing will ever trump direct relationship.

No article can adequately communicate someone's heart.

No photo can show a full picture of someone's life.

No post can express the totality of someone's worldview.

But conversations with people who directly know a person give life and breath to that person, even if they're far away.

Take your time.

Do your research.

Ask questions.

You might just discover someone in your field who comes from a bad family and isn't from your area but works hard and has a good reputation.

You're welcome.

THOUGHTS FROM A THERAPIST

Dr. Deb on Internet "Stalking"

Like any good thing, we can take the benefits and overdo them, making the outcome more harmful than helpful. This can easily be applied to internet stalking. In a study conducted in early 2018, the Pew Research Center found that one quarter of Americans are online "almost constantly" and an additional 43 percent of Americans are online several times a day. Researchers have also found a significant relationship between social media use among young adults and rising rates of depression.[1]

Social media and the internet have provided us with significant access to information, and as a result, the world has become smaller and smaller. As Bianca states, this provides ample opportunity for research and acceptable "stalking," but it's only half the picture. Our online platforms can also provide ample opportunity for obsessive stalking and over-comparison. The problem with online information is that it's always limited. We see a Facebook picture of the guy we like with his arms around a girl, and we immediately assume she's his girlfriend (or maybe even that he's a "player"). Rarely is the first thought that she is his sister or cousin.

When we only have access to one side of any information, it's easy to fill in the blanks with our own interpretation of what we're seeing. And once we get started down the rabbit hole of desperately trying to fill in the blanks, it's hard to stop. It's the Alice-in-Wonderland effect; you've found yourself stuck in a curated fantasyland.

So how do you set yourself up to engage in acceptable stalking without crossing over to obsessive stalking? Set your expectations and limitations before you start your research. Here are two tips:

1. **BE PURPOSEFUL IN ESTABLISHING YOUR GOALS.** If your objective is to investigate someone's interests, connections, and overall visual presence, stay committed to that pursuit and only that pursuit. Don't log on to aimlessly find out anything and everything you can about that guy you met at the coffee shop yesterday. The next thing you know, three hours have gone by and you've discovered that he is, in fact, not an unemployed hippie hitchhiker with three wives and a dozen mismatched kids but a missionary photographer who regularly travels overseas to document the work of agencies with which he partners. At least, that's the story you're telling yourself.

2. **LIMIT THE AMOUNT OF TIME YOU'RE GOING TO SPEND RESEARCHING UP FRONT.** Smart phones, smart watches, and smart tablets can also provide smart boundaries. Be intentional and set a timer. If you've given one hour to finding John Doe's online footprint and all it has revealed is his current job, favorite food, regular summer lake vacation with extended family, and his adorable obsession with his rescue pup, that's a great starting point. The last thing you want to do is show up for date number one already knowing everything there is to know about the guy. A little mystery is still a good thing.

CHAPTER 2

CLEANLINESS IS NEXT
TO MARRIEDNESS

*"Wash, put on perfume, and get dressed in your best
clothes. Then go down to the threshing floor."*
RUTH 3:3

During my junior year of high school, I was captain of the varsity soccer team. I was the first on the field and the last to leave. Come what may—rain, heat, or high school heartbreak—my goal was to lead the team well. Our goalkeeper had an idea after a three-game winning streak: stop shaving.

"We have been slaughtering the other teams, and I don't want to be superstitious, but let's keep the pattern going by not shaving our legs," she said. With state finals a serious possibility, we all agreed to look intimidating (and hairy).

Three weeks into our Samson vow (not letting a razor come near us), I saw our team bonding over how long our leg hair had gotten and how frightening we looked.

Then Coach Frank pulled me aside and asked why all the girls looked so slovenly. He quoted Deion Sanders, saying, "If you look good, you feel good. If you feel good, you play good." I examined the team while they were setting up the equipment on the field and realized we all looked like creatures awakening from hibernation: matted hair, dirty jerseys, and leg hair we could possibly braid. We looked rough, and not in an athletic way.

Quick to defend my team, I explained our pact and believed Coach Frank would give me a high five. Instead, he told me we looked horrible. "Bianca," he said in a hushed voice, "everything about you says something about you. If you don't take yourself seriously, no one will."

Perhaps it was not only *what* he said, but *how* he said it that jolted me out of cluelessness. I immediately saw my team differently. If we rolled up to our next game looking like prehistoric mastodons, we wouldn't be intimidating, we would be embarrassing. After practice I decided we would all shave our legs, wear matching team hair bows, and have our jerseys properly cleaned. In time for our next game, we shaved off our superstition (and our leg hair), and then made it to the state championship semifinals.

The church is often pretty quiet when it comes to addressing the importance of physical care. When we do hear preaching about the physical, the words shared are usually pulled out of 1 Samuel 16:7: "People look at the outward appearance, but the LORD looks at the heart."

What a sigh of relief and comfort in a world that constantly barrages women with the ideology that we will never be enough. We have a God who looks at our heart versus a number on a scale or a bra size.

Of course, what God told Samuel was true. God looks at the heart, but that doesn't remove the fact that humans still look at what's on the outside. Rather than speaking about physical appearance (I'm no stylist or fashionista, so I leave that to the professionals), I want to address physical *maintenance*.

There is a difference between vanity and maintenance.

Imagine a car. If you own a car, you know there are certain things that must be done regularly to ensure the car will run properly—tune-ups, oil changes, filter replacements—that's maintenance. But if you want to drop the car, slap some rims on the tires, and tint the windows, that won't improve how the car functions, only how it looks—that's vanity.

I'm all for owning my shape, blessing my body, and declaring that I am fearfully and wonderfully made. But we create a damaging narrative when we confuse self-love and acceptance with an excuse to let ourselves go.

Whether it is living the mommy life, the single life, or the I've-stopped-caring life, we might need to have a conversation. (Please know I say this completely in love. You can ask any of my friends, family, or staff: the conversation I'm having with you is one I have had before. I'm discussing this not just to help you, but also to make you accountable. You can never say I didn't tell you.)

I had a chat a year ago with a young woman I genuinely loved. Stacy was smart, educated, and goal-oriented. She was also single and working a dead-end job. Over coffee she explained to me that she really wanted to step into adulthood with confidence but didn't know why doors weren't opening.

She was wearing jeans with holes, tattered flip-flops, ill-fitting glasses, and it looked like she hadn't washed her hair in a few too many days. I personally didn't mind because it was an informal coffee date, but she was talking to me in a way that hinted she wanted a job working for *me*. Or, at the very least, she was hinting that I might possibly connect her with great organizations that might find her skills useful. However, nothing about her or her disposition indicated *professional*, *successful*, or *ambitious*.

As I listened, I and all my multiple personalities were fighting with each other inside my head! The conversation went something like this:

Kind Bianca: Just listen to her and nod your head in understanding.

Savage Bianca: Are you really not going to keep it real right now? Someone needs to tell her the truth.

Compassionate Bianca: She just needs someone to hug and encourage her.

Blatantly Honest Bianca: She cannot be taken seriously with that ketchup stain on her shirt!

Christian Bianca: Jesus loves her just the way she is.

Carnal Bianca: TELL HER NO ONE IS LIKE JESUS AND SHE NEEDS TO WASH HER HAIR.

After a half hour of listening to her wallow in sorrow, the war waging within me was too much, and I blurted out, "Everything about you says something about you." It was just like my coach had said to me fifteen years earlier: if you don't take yourself seriously, no one else will.

She explained that her life was busy, and she just wanted people to love and accept her as she was. I affirmed her sentiment, but then explained that we have to put forth *effort*. Expecting or demanding to be accepted without effort is unrealistic. Not everyone will hire you. Not everyone will love you. Not everyone will want to be your friend. So show up at your best and slowly allow yourself to be vulnerable enough to reveal your worst.

Ever so gently, we began to discuss the importance of personal hygiene, dressing for the job you want, and letting someone know you're available and interested in dating. Sweet Stacy received these words and began to understand the difference between physical maintenance and vanity.

Ruth, like my friend Stacy, was a woman who was so busy working and taking care of others that she might have forgotten to put herself on her list of priorities. I get it. It happens to the best of us, including the selfless Ruth.

After working in the field for months, another harvest season came to a close, and Boaz hosted what we would consider an end-of-the-year party—a big night for his workers to celebrate all the hard labor done in the field.

Naomi had seen her beloved Ruth wake up early, throw her hair in a messy bun, and grab some barley toast as she ran out the door to get to work. When she returned home late in the evening, she was exhausted, dirty, and probably smelling a bit ripe.

With every rising and setting sun, Naomi realized Ruth was getting older, and she worried that her daughter-in-law would be left in a foreign country without a penny to her name. She started an honest conversation out of love and concern:

> One day Ruth's mother-in-law Naomi said to her, "My daughter, I must find a home for you, where you will be well provided for. Now Boaz, with whose women you have worked, is a relative of ours. Tonight he will be winnowing barley on the thresh-ing floor. Wash, put on perfume, and get dressed in your best clothes." (Ruth 3:1–3)

Did you catch what she did there? Don't miss the clear direc-tive in this text. Naomi told Ruth to take care of herself, instructing her to do three things:

1. Wash Yo' Self
2. Anoint Yo' Self
3. Change Yo' Clothes

Ruth had lost her husband. Maybe her self-care began to deteriorate as a result of that experience. In any case, Naomi noticed, and moved to give her daughter-in-law some necessary guidance.

Now, I could take this moment to give you a laundry list of worldly beauty standards and expectations, but you've no doubt heard too much of that already. Instead, let me expound on (read: Biancafy) what Mama Naomi said to Ruth.

Wash Yo' Self!

Naomi to Ruth: Oy vey! Daughter, you smell like fermented barley and sweat. Go hop in the shower, shave your armpits, and wash all your cracks.

Young mothers, college students, and busy women everywhere, can we please make a pact to shower at *least* every other day? I know this might feel like a stretch for some (and it might be vomit-inducing to others who religiously bathe twice a day), but if we all agree to set a standard, it might help our sisters keep the hygiene bar set high.

Listen, there is no judgment in this conversation. Life happens, and sometimes we are so exhausted we're forced to decide: sleep or shower?

As you wrestle through this decision, may I remind you that though your scent might be enjoyed by your significant others, musk and fermented cheese are acquired tastes, just like our body odor? Be kind to everyone in the universe and make sure you are odor-checking frequently.

I'm not saying this to be judgmental. I say this because there have been days when I got a whiff of a cross-country trucker and shockingly realized it was *me*. So for the sake of humanity and my pride, I shower every day and keep breath mints nearby, deodorant in my car, and perfume in my purse.

Lastly, for my sisters who don't like to wash their hair, dry shampoo will only get you so far. Stop believing the commercials.

If people are concerned to light a candle around you for fear of catching your greasy hair on fire, it might be a sign your oily hair needs to be deep cleaned. Set the standard and maintain your mane.

Anoint Yo' Self!

Naomi to Ruth: Listen, Ruthie, I want you to smell like
the rose of Sharon, like a lily of the valley, so go borrow
some of that perfume I use for special occasions.

In Hebrew culture, mourning over the death of a loved one usually lasts for thirty days (*shloshim*). During this period, the bereaved wear mourning clothes, they don't use lotions, oils, or perfumes, and they abstain from engaging in dating relationships. While a month is customary, the practice of *shloshim* can last up to a year.

After she was widowed, Ruth became a manual laborer and would no doubt have been exhausted every day after long hours in the fields. We can safely assume that Ruth made little to no attempt to spruce herself up.

It's possible Ruth really just needed a long bath and a little fragrance for the party. But maybe Naomi was releasing Ruth from her time of mourning and giving her permission to love again.

Either way, Naomi encouraged Ruth to invest in some solid self-care. Don't believe me? Showering is a necessity, but perfume is a luxury. Naomi told Ruth to do **both**. There is nothing wrong with doing a few things that make you feel and look fabulous. As Naomi gave Ruth permission to feel beautiful, I believe we have that same permission.

Remember, there is a big difference between self-*care* and self-*ish*. Social critics chide this generation for being obsessed with memes, avocado toast, and selfies. But research is beginning to show that millennials might actually be the generation of emotional intelligence.

Self-care existed millennia before millennials did. Ancient Greeks saw it as a way to make people more honest citizens and more likely to care for others. More recently, Audre Lorde said, "Caring for myself is not self-indulgence, it is self-preservation."

Dr. Anabel Bejarano, in her article "Self-Care for Women: Now Not Later," argues that recharging is essential to women for their mental, emotional, physical, and spiritual well-being. Women who practice self-care suffer less from anxiety, depression, and stress-related diseases, including heart disease, the leading cause of death for women in the US.

But before you bust out the credit card and break the bank on nightly baths in pure Evian water, let me clarify that self-care doesn't mean being opulent. For Ruth, it was simply using some perfume. For you, it might mean going for a jog, getting a manicure, or taking an indulgent soak in the tub.

By and large, self-care is free. Dr. Bejarano suggests the following as a guide to help us maintain or start recharging:

- Be responsible for your body: sleep, eat nourishing food, and exercise.
- Take care of yourself: take a bath, complete your yearly physical, tend to medical issues in a timely manner.
- Treat yourself with compassion: don't listen to negative people or critical self-thoughts.
- Create fun: hang out with friends, produce art, start a sport or hobby.
- Expand your mind: read books, discover new methods of organizing, study a new discipline. (Bonus: research shows this slows down the aging process!)

Change Yo' Clothes!

Naomi to Ruth: Remember that beautiful party dress you wore when
you and my son would go out? Put that on! You'll look beautiful.

In Bethlehem, Ruth and Naomi had only what they could carry back from Moab, and I doubt either of them was heaving a giant wardrobe trunk. It's quite possible that Ruth was still in mourning rags given the untimely and unexpected death of her husband. At the very least, we can say that whatever Ruth was wearing was probably tattered from her long days in the fields.

Sweating like a pig and working like an ox, Ruth had only been seen wearing her faded Target mom jeans, beat-up running shoes, and a T-shirt she won at a carnival in Moab (or something along those lines—I told you this would be Biancafied!). Naomi knew Ruth's standard outfit wasn't doing her any favors, so she wisely told Ruth to go ahead and get dolled up. In other words, care about her clothes.

You don't need to be rich to look presentable. I say this with authority because I grew up poor and never, ever owned designer clothes. Who am I kidding? Almost everything I wore was a donation or a hand-me-down. But that was never an excuse to look sloppy or lazy! (Allow me to tell you about the time I forgot to put lotion on my legs before church and my mom made me lick my hand and rub moisture onto my legs to take away the ashy look around my knees. My mama did NOT mess around when it came to appearance.)

Don't be intimidated by fashion bloggers and Instagram stylists! More than being opulent or excessive, be clean and resourceful.

When Matt and I got married, we were on a strict budget (when you marry a missions pastor, you hear things like, "Bianca, a designer handbag is a WANT, not a NEED!"), so I had to go back to my roots and start living on a prayer. Me and Bon Jovi, right? Here are three easy and simple ways to live on a fashion budget:

Consignment and Thrift Stores

After a quick Google search, I found some great consignment stores and began donating my old clothes and picking up new items for little to no cost. (If you don't know what a consignment store is, it's basically a really fancy thrift store where you can sell items. You're welcome.) One of my favorite handbags, which I still use today, is a Tom Ford steal I found at a local consignment store. If you are patient, you can find some amazing bargains!

Recycling

I had a pair of designer jeans I bought when I was single, impulsive, and budget-free. I loved them, and after years of wear they remained in good shape, but their color was fading. One trip to Target and one bottle of clothing dye later, my jeans were a dark black again. Voilà! Good as new!

Confidence

There's no designer, tailor, or haute couture gown that can make an insecure girl look confident, and confidence is *beautiful*. Whether you are big ballin' or on a budget, wear your clothes proudly! If your body ain't built like a supermodel, own your curves! Even if all you have is your smile, grin wide and sparkle, baby!

You are a child of God with a purpose for your life. Your confidence isn't going to come from a clothing label, thigh gap, or designer handbag. Your confidence will come in understanding that it isn't what you wear, but *whose you are*!

No matter what, you can steal my reminder that I stole from Naomi: shower, shave, and sparkle!

THOUGHTS FROM A THERAPIST

Dr. Deb on Self-Care

It's safe to say that self-care behavior can readily produce or enhance more affirmative emotional experiences. Naomi's instruction that Ruth attend to her appearance and presentation might be easily interpreted as being for the benefit of Boaz, but perhaps there's more to the story. Ruth, a widow with the exhausting burden of manual labor, was likely to return home each day feeling drained, depleted, and insecure. Her sweaty, disheveled, tattered appearance would serve to reinforce an emotional connection to this reality and put Ruth at risk of self-reinforcing a false identity, one that might cause her to believe she was unworthy. Instead, Naomi's direction suggests something different. Wash, put on a pleasant aroma, and dress nicely, because you ARE worthy. Perhaps these actions didn't change Ruth's emotions or thoughts immediately, but the disciplined action of taking time to invest in herself would directly contradict any deceptive judgments that she wasn't worthy of such investments.

CHAPTER 3

WANT THE WOO

*At mealtime Boaz said to her, "Come over here.
Have some bread and dip it in the wine vinegar."
When she sat down with the harvesters, he offered
her some roasted grain. She ate all she wanted and
had some left over.*

RUTH 2:14

"I just don't know what's wrong with me. I'm always attracting guys who either don't know or don't care that women want romance. I want to feel special! Is it too much to ask for a guy to pick up a phone and ask me out on a date? Are my standards too high?"

I've known Lauren for over a decade. She is a sweet brunette who loves dogs, traveling, and running marathons. She's also in her midthirties, has never been married, and hasn't been in a relationship for the last seven years.

Lauren had a unique knack for attracting—shall we say— *interesting* guys. Guys who were emotionally unavailable, obsessively involved in online war games, or who lived in their mothers' basements with a few too many action figures. We joked and called it her spiritual gift. Lauren had been on a string of bad dates when she met Chris at a casual gathering at a friend's house. She sat next to him, and they talked the whole night. When she got home, she discovered that he'd starting following her on social media.

Now, before you think this is something special, intentional, unique, or romantic, STOP. This is not romantic. It's basic. In this day and age, a social media follow might indicate interest, curiosity, or just plain creepiness, and it's nothing a potential landlord wouldn't do if you filled out an application to rent. Trust me, and keep reading.

Lauren woke up the next morning to discover that Chris had replied to a photo she posted of herself, exhausted with her dog, after a long walk. He direct messaged this reply:

"Ha thats cool"

Just that. No apostrophe, no comma, no punctuation, just a lame half-sentence that was grammatically incorrect. *AND SHE WAS EXCITED?!* She responded back with a dog emoji and replied, "I know, right? My dog is so cute. Do you have a dog?"

Lauren's simple reply led to a string of direct messages. Their communication went on for a couple of weeks, complete with memes, gifs, and emojis. At some point they realized, coincidentally, they would be at the same concert in a few days. (Thank you, social media, for allowing us to creep into people's lives and discover their every move!)

Lauren suggested they meet up at the concert and hang out afterward. His reply: "cool." (Just that. No capitalization, no punctuation, just a lame half-sentence that was grammatically incorrect. Again.)

Let's pause and take inventory:

- Lauren initiated the conversation with Chris at their friend's house.
- Chris direct messaged her a reply on social media.

- Lauren initiated their social media conversations.
- Chris sent a general post for his 783 followers about going to a concert.
- Lauren saw his post and initiated the meet-up at the concert.

Are we seeing a pattern here?

Lauren complained that she attracted guys who didn't seem intentional or capable of moving forward in relationships. But she wasn't doing anything to make them want or need to initiate. She wasn't even giving them space to initiate.

On a bright Saturday afternoon shortly after the concert, Lauren and I met up for a run along the beach. I want to say it was a great workout, but that would hardly be accurate. We stopped constantly because I was either laughing too hard from her recounting the dates she'd been on or grabbing her phone to read through the Instagrammed conversations.

When we finally completed our run, we sat down to stretch on a bench overlooking the Pacific Ocean. Through laughter and eventually tears, she told me that once they'd met up at the concert, Chris seemed to be on his phone constantly. She tried making conversation, but the music was loud, and communication felt strained. Halfway through the show, she peered over his arm to see what was vying for his attention. Much to her surprise and frustration, he was direct messaging *other women* while at the concert with her.

At the end of the night, Lauren told Chris she had to work in the morning and thought it best she head home. When she lay down on her bed to check her phone, Chris had DM'd her a sleepy-face emoji. That's it. Not even a single grammatically incorrect half-sentence.

She recounted this exchange as she gazed out over the ocean, and then said the words I recounted above: "They say there are more fish in the sea, but I just don't know what's wrong with me. I'm always attracting guys who either don't know or don't care that women want romance. I want to feel special! Is it too much to ask for a guy to pick up a phone and ask me out on a date? Are my standards too high?"

Lauren certainly isn't the only single lady who has felt this way. I've spoken to many women who seem to constantly ask themselves the daunting and elusive question, "Is it me?" In response, I'd like to point out that we are all uniquely fashioned. We are created differently with individually attractive qualities and purposes, so the short and general answer is a resounding *no*. You are not the problem. But if you are willing to accept unacceptable behavior, that is a very big problem.

I will confidently say that not only is it okay to want to be wooed, we are hardwired for it. God gave us the desire to be wanted and cared for by another human being. WANT THE WOO! This does not mean we should be codependent or needy. It simply means that God, in His infinite wisdom, knew that it was not good for people to live isolated and alone (Genesis 2:18).

Boaz was a man just like any man today. But he possessed an awareness that many single brothers we meet on the daily still need to learn. Please know I'm not lambasting or shaming men. There are a number of factors that inform why some men aren't the greatest at proper interaction in personal relationships (divorced homes, missing parents, culture shifts, poor instructions, being raised by a pack of wolves—the list goes on), but it's never too late to teach our friends, sons, boyfriends, and coworkers how we would like to be treated.

Just so I'm sure you understand me, we are the ones who set the standard for the treatment we receive. In other words, **people will only treat us in ways we allow ourselves to be treated.**

Lauren wanted a phone call and a proper invitation for a date, but she continued to entertain conversations via Facebook Messenger and Instagram. Then, she took it upon herself to ask for a casual meet-up, when what she really hoped for was a one-on-one date. Do you see what was happening there? The things she accepted from Chris weren't in line with the things she wanted from him. She taught him that DMs and lackadaisical one-liners were okay with her, and his behavior fell in line. In a way, she got exactly what she asked for. The poor girl never stood a chance.

People will only treat us in ways we allow ourselves to be treated.

When it comes to dating, according to Dr. Deb, we are quick to get pulled into the emotional thinking part of our brain. Rational thought flies right out the window, and we end up making decisions based on our feelings in the moment. Don't get me wrong, sometimes those feelings are the BEST part of new relationships—the giddy, goofy, butterflies-in-your-stomach feelings. However, we can also make some pretty ridiculous choices when the fleeting feelings of eagerness, excitement, and anticipation show up at the beginning of a first encounter with a cute *possibility*.

In the moment, Lauren's rational perspective of wanting the woo was lost in the emotional whirlwind of excitement brought on by the mere possibility of interest: "Ha thats cool."

Decisions that are based on emotions aren't inherently bad, but emotions often lack the perspective we need to exercise wisdom. "We need both emotional *and* rational thinking to make choices that are healthy and consistent with our values," says Dr. Deb. "For Lauren, that would look like acknowledging the exhilaration that comes from someone showing even initial interest but *balancing* that with her rational value of wanting intentional pursuit from a potential boyfriend."

Let's see what we can learn about this subject from Ruth and Boaz.

He invited her to spend some time.

At mealtime Boaz said to her, "Come over here. Have some bread and dip it in the wine vinegar." When she sat down with the harvesters, he offered her some roasted grain. She ate all she wanted and had some left over. (Ruth 2:14)

Do you see what Boaz did there?

He said, "Come over here." When a man invites you into his space, he is taking initiative. And before you think my head is in the Victorian Age when a woman sat idly by and waited for a man to *choose* her, read chapter 7 on women taking initiative and thank me later. What I *am* saying is we can learn something from Boaz in terms of social cues and when someone might be interested.

We certainly can't all be relationship experts, but we can be experts at picking up on social cues. Asking someone out is a brave act, risking rejection and putting ourselves in a very vulnerable position. So if someone takes initiative, take note. Don't get all crazy and start picking out your future children's names, but be aware that he might be interested in getting to know you if he's willing to put himself out there.

Before you jump into a relationship, invite your potential partner into *your* space to assess how he will engage in a work space, play space, or friend space. This will allow you to get to know someone from a slight distance and observe how he engages with the people in your world.

Within the first week of dating, Matt (who became my husband) invited me to hang out with him and his best friend. I thought it was a bit weird, and I felt really intimidated, but Matt explained later that it was a vetting process. If he was caught up in his emotions, he feared he wouldn't make a wise decision. Having his best friend get to see us interact (and grill me on every topic under the sun) allowed Matt to have someone else weigh in on our compatibility and chemistry.

He invited her to lunch.

"Have some bread and dip it in the wine vinegar."

Don't miss that! He fed her. It may be true that the way to a man's heart is through his stomach, but Boaz knew the way to a woman's heart was bread, y'all. (And can I get an AMEN from my carb-loving sisters?!)

Boaz invited Ruth into his space, then gave her something to eat. Please note that he didn't touch her or expect a make-out session because he bought her a meal. He was offering her a meal out of the kindness of his heart. *That* is the type of man you want to go out with.

It's all too common these days for men and women to date with the expectation that if a guy is so generous as to bankroll a nice meal, there has to be some kind of catch—some physical or sexual obligation. Let me be completely unequivocal here, friends. I would sooner condone you grabbing the steak knife and threatening castration than see you fold to the pressure of our culture—or your date—to get physical just because he paid for your meal!

You are worth more than a T-bone steak and maple-glazed carrots at a nice restaurant. He ain't having you for dessert until there are a different kind of karats involved. HELLO, homegirl. Know your worth. You can buy your own dinner, and as I always say, *No ringy, no dingy!*

He introduced her to his community.

"When she sat down with the harvesters, he offered her some roasted grain."

Boaz invited Ruth to sit with his community—his coworkers. And she accepted.

Have you ever dated someone who never introduced you to his family or friends? Have you been the one to keep a guy from your inner circle? There's something very necessary about sharing basic elements of normal life with your significant other, even at the beginning of a relationship. If you're not willing to take a guy to meet your besties, examine what you might feel is lacking enough to keep you holding him at arm's length. On the flip side, if he's doing the same, you might need to ask yourself why. I'm not saying you should expect to meet his mother as soon as you've agreed to a second date, but if he's willing to open up about family and begin to invite you to hang with friends or meet coworkers, it's generally a sign he wants to at least see whether you might make sense in his life.

Don't overanalyze it, and stop putting pressure on yourself. Go out on a date! Relax! An invitation to coffee isn't a marriage proposal! Enjoy a meal with someone! Meet their friends! Use exclamation marks! Life is too short to be weird.

He was generous with what he had.

"She ate all she wanted and had some left over."

Boaz didn't hold anything back in the meal he gave to Ruth. Scripture tells us she ate all she wanted. Keep in mind, Ruth and Naomi didn't have much. They had left Moab widowed and empty-handed. Ruth was forced to find work in the fields just to make ends meet and would have been starving by the time everyone was breaking for lunch. And I'm not talking about some arbitrary juice fast moment when we're an hour in and that next apple/carrot/beet blend ain't coming until noon so we whine and moan that we're *just starving*! Ruth had very little choice in the matter—her hunger was legit.

Boaz offered Ruth bread and grain, and handed out unlimited dipping sauces like she was at Chick-fil-A! Ruth, meanwhile, ate "all she wanted." Generosity is a quality that bodes well in most aspects of a person's life. I certainly am not encouraging y'all to be greedy little gold diggers, but pay attention to how a date gives. If he's generous with you, with your waiter, with his time, with your family and friends, it's a sign he's a stand-up individual. Read the signs, ladies!

AND side note: Ruth chowed down and still managed to land her man! If we learn from her example, we won't be afraid to eat on a date. In our early stages of dating, Matt took me to a beautiful restaurant in Newport Beach. Too nervous to order something I would normally eat, I ordered a *side salad*. Not as an appetizer—*as my entree*. What a waste of a good meal! It's silly to pretend you're satisfied with a plain chicken breast and some steamed broccoli when you know you're really a gal who loves to throw down pepperoni pizza and root beer. Eat how you would normally eat, sister. (That said, it may be advisable to avoid anything super drippy, sloppy, or likely to get stuck in your teeth on a first date. You know, so you don't look like a total animal. But hey, do you.)

We can't deny it. Boaz honored Ruth, invited her to sit with his community, and fed her well. This is what I call *wooing a woman*. Boaz knew the way to honor a woman and her inherent value.

A haphazard half-sentence like "ha thats cool" doesn't honor you. So can we institute a general rule that limits direct message conversations? If conversations remain restricted to texts and DMs and never progress to real life, it might indicate a lack of interest or initiative. If no one pulls the trigger to take things to the next level, keep it moving.

To clarify, not all women care about proper grammar. I'm a writer, so it's important for me to date someone who knows the difference between *there*, *their*, and *they're*. What I **do** want to advocate for is proper communication and strategies for you to adequately get to know someone. I want you to want the woo!

Here's my mantra for you: No woo? No way!

THOUGHTS FROM A THERAPIST

Dr. Deb on Values and Dating

If you want to attract the right kind of guy, you have to make a commitment to say no to the wrong kind of guy or to your own misguided behaviors.

1. **KNOW YOUR VALUES WHEN IT COMES TO DATING AND MEN.** Share them with your community, the people you trust, and be open to insight, feedback, and accountability. If you have clear expectations, you'll set yourself up to make healthy choices when the emotional center of your brain is flooded with euphoria because that hot guy in front of you in the coffee shop line simply turns around and smiles.

2. **DON'T SHIFT YOUR VALUES TO MAKE SOMETHING HAPPEN THAT'S NOT IN LINE WITH YOUR EXPECTATIONS.** Don't justify your actions to achieve some end result. Your values are valuable, and justification almost always ends in disappointment and regret.

3. **BE INTENTIONAL IN DEFINING WHAT YOU WANT *BEFORE* YOU MEET HOTTIE-IN-COFFEE-SHOP, AND THEN KEEP YOUR ACTIONS CONSISTENT WITH YOUR DESIRES.** Take purposeful pauses at the beginning of any getting-to-know-you stage. Reflect on where you are and what you're seeing, and evaluate the experience through the lens of your values. Make your commitment now to *want the woo*.

If you start conversing with someone on social media and want to get to know him, move to exchanging numbers and start communicating like adults. Pick up a phone, call to make plans, and plan a date (maybe even at a restaurant that has cloth napkins and doesn't use plastic sporks as cutlery). If you initiate the date, great. But make sure there is reciprocity and investment on his side, too! Make him work for your heart. You are worth that kind of work. Act like it.

If your behavior is inconsistent with your values, you could end up in a relationship that only exists in inboxes and text messages like some chick-on-the-side that no one wants to claim in public. Your phone can also be used to talk. So if it doesn't ring, then *delete contact*. By the same token, if you find yourself someplace swanky and realize it's only a setup by a man in pursuit of some early action, put your steak down and leave the restaurant.

Check, please!

Now let's take a personal inventory . . .

Answer these questions:

1. When was the last time you communicated with a guy regularly on social media for longer than two weeks?
2. Who initiated the conversations?
3. Was there depth and interest in getting to know you, or did it feel like a hookup?

If you've realized some unhealthy patterns in your communication, adjust your sails and go find the other fish in the sea!

CHAPTER 4

FIND A MAN WHO LOVES TO GIVE GIFTS

He also said, "Bring me the shawl you are wearing
and hold it out." When she did so, he poured into it
six measures of barley and placed the bundle on her.
RUTH 3:15

Listen friends, I know I'm fearfully and wonderfully made. I know I was knit in my mother's womb by the hand of God, and he foreordained the width of my waist and the thickness of my thighs. I believe God created me in infinite love and thought his workmanship was beautiful. But let's get one thing straight: I've never had guys craning their heads out of car windows to holler at me. I never had to turn down a date because I was already booked on a Friday night. In all my years of existence, I was never torn between two or three men who were fighting for my affections.

My dating life was like a hunt for a pirate's buried treasure. Every now and again, I'd think I'd found the elusive treasure chest, only to discover it was empty . . . and had mommy issues. (Okay, so maybe my illustration broke down a little, but one day

I'll tell you about the time I went on a date with a guy who picked me up in his mom's car, then called her to ask where we should go to dinner and what he should order for dinner. Awkward.)

When Destiny called to ask me for dating advice, I was confused. We were about the same age, but that's where our commonalities ended. I knew her sister, Chastity, because she had attended a summer Bible study I was teaching on Song of Songs (an Old Testament book about romance and dating written by King Solomon). Every Tuesday night at my dad's church in East Los Angeles, I'd round up five hundred young women for a Bible study on sex, dating, romance, and conflict resolution. (In hindsight, I find this absolutely hilarious because, at the time, I was a single, twenty-seven-year-old virgin who hadn't dated in five years. The irony is beyond me!)

Destiny worked as a model and actress in Los Angeles, but because of her work schedule, she couldn't attend the Bible study. Chastity, loving sister that she was, faithfully recorded the teachings and sent them to Destiny each week. It was through this exchange that I ultimately wound up meeting with Destiny for coffee and a chat.

With a name like Destiny, you can probably conjure up a mental image of her fabulosity. She was tall with a flowing mane of jet-black hair that reached to the curve of her lower back. There was an ethnic ambiguity in her almond eyes and dark skin, and I witnessed many men suffer whiplash just to get a longer look at her as we walked down Cahuenga Boulevard and into a small Hollywood café. Destiny was breathtakingly stunning. I felt the eyes of others watching her every move, including mine. I wasn't sure why we were meeting, but I couldn't wait to find out.

"Bianca, I really need help with my dating life," she said, fighting back tears.

What I wanted to say: "ME TOO, HOMEGIRL! Jesus, fix it!"

What I said: "Really? Tell me more."

Through choked sniffles and tears, she explained that finding a good, godly, Christian man in Hollywood was like finding a needle in a haystack. I took her analogy and ran with it. "It's like finding free parking in LA at 9 a.m.! It's like finding a leprechaun in a field of four-leaf clovers! It's like finding a unicorn on a road of cotton candy!" I always take things too far, but at least Destiny laughed.

She explained that there was one guy in particular—a colleague, Ben—who seemed to like her, but she questioned his intentions because he seemed to constantly shower her with gifts. She'd started to avoid him because she worried that his gifts would be tied to expectations, and she wasn't sure what those expectations might be. She spewed out a series of questions in rapid succession: "What if Ben expects me to already be won over by his presents? What if he wants something in return? What if I discover I don't like him, and I accepted all his gifts? Doesn't that make me a gold digger?"

Though I'm not a relationship expert or trained therapist, I do believe God has given me wisdom to see situations plainly. I listened intently and tried to understand where she was coming from.

Her questions were fair. Totally fair. But if she thought Ben was a good guy, if his gifts were thoughtful and his actions were respectful, wasn't she denying herself the opportunity to get to know someone potentially amazing? I didn't want Destiny to miss out on the chance to connect with a generous, godly, Christian man because she was afraid she might not like him or worried that accepting his gifts would involuntarily send the wrong message. "What if gifts are his love language?" I asked innocently. She gave me a quizzical look, and I realized she hadn't read Gary Chapman's life-changing book, *The Five Love Languages*. I quickly explained that giving gifts is one of five principal ways individuals express care for the people in their lives.

Now, if Ben's gifts were cars, lingerie, or luxury handbags, that would have raised some flags for me. Major expenses (unless this dude had a money tree) would seem too big an investment in a barely-there relationship. He hadn't even been clear about his feelings yet. If he was inappropriately suggestive, surprising her with lacy nighties from Victoria's Secret, I'd have been certain he was after only one thing. But Ben's small tokens and gestures were little ways of expressing his care for Destiny. He brought her coffee at work. He invited her to lunch (and paid for it). He bought her new running shoes because he knew she was training for a marathon.

I wanted to empathize and join her in her consternation like a good girlfriend would do, but I just couldn't affirm her fear. I said, "Destiny, he's from Idaho. He's simple and sturdy and smart and saved. I'm not sure he has some master plan to manipulate you or force you to date him because he paid for lunch. What if he just wants to show you what you are worth to him?"

Though their backstories are a little different, Ben was like a modern-day Boaz. Generous, kind, compassionate, and concerned for the well-being of a woman he cared for.

> He also said, "Bring me the shawl you are wearing and hold it out." When she did so, he poured into it six measures of barley and placed the bundle on her. (Ruth 3:15)

If Destiny was concerned about Ben's gifts, she would've died twice over with gifts from Boaz. Boaz gave Ruth six measures of barley—that's anywhere from 75 to 150 pounds of barley as a gift for her to take home! Not only did Ruth receive an incredible gift, but she also received a workout, as she had to carry that bundle all the way home.

Gifts can carry a lot of meaning, and it's good to consider the motivation behind them. However, problems can arise when we make assumptions about the purpose of someone's gift before we really know the facts. Russell Belk and Gregory Coon, two of the leading researchers on gift-giving, define three typical motivations behind the giving of gifts: economic exchange, social exchange, and the expression of agape love. Economic exchange suggests that the gift comes with some expectation of a return on investment. There's an anticipation on the part of the gift-giver that their gift will earn them a "reward" (another date, a good-night kiss, or something more).

If you have reason to believe there's an expectation of some sort along with the gift you've been given, that's a red flag! Again, repeat these words after me: "No ringy, no dingy. No ringy, no dingy!" A gift motivated by social exchange means the giver wants to communicate meaning and commitment to the relationship. It's kind of the equivalent of a guy saying, "Hey, I'm interested in you! Let's make something happen here!" Agape exchange is selfless; the gift comes with no strings attached. The gift is given just because.

It's definitely okay to consider the why behind a gift, but remember: the expectation that a gift will earn some type of physical reward is only one of the possible motivations. Jumping to this assumption eliminates the possibility that you've actually got a guy who's simply trying to tell you, "I think you're special."

What's more, Harvard psychology professor Ellen J. Langer offers the insight that *not* accepting gifts doesn't help a relationship; giving to others reinforces our feelings for them and makes us feel effective and caring. "If I don't let you give me a gift," she says, "then I'm not encouraging you to think about me and think about things I like. I am preventing you from experiencing the joy of engaging in all those activities. You do people a disservice by not giving them the gift of giving."[1]

The last time I heard from Destiny, she sent me a card and a baby announcement. After our chat in Hollywood, Ben and Destiny went on their first date, and as most fairytales end, they lived happily ever after. I will always treasure the handwritten note she sent:

Dear Bianca: We wanted you to see the fruit of our union and let you know why we named our daughter Diara. Her name means *gift*. Not only is she a gift to us, but you played a role in me understanding how Ben shows affection by giving gifts. Now we created a gift together.

The only way this could've gotten better is if they'd given Diara the middle name BIANCA! But I digress. I was so excited for Destiny and Ben.

If Destiny had never let her guard down and accepted the genuine sentiment behind Ben's gifts, she would never have gone on that first date with him. She would never have discovered that gifts, in fact, were his love language or known that he asked about her when he saw her at church. She wouldn't have learned that he prayed for her and heaped spiritual blessings on her from afar. She had to accept that his generosity was heartfelt. It took a lot for him to work up the courage to bring her coffee at work. And because of it, she learned the power of giving, both for the giver and the one who receives.

If you're not familiar with it already, Gary Chapman's *The Five Love Languages* is a game-changing read. Gift-giving is only one of the major categories he outlines on how people show love. If someone in your life doesn't happen to be a gift-giver but, say, heaps you with kind words and compliments (words of affirmation), gives generously of his time (quality time), does thoughtful things for you (acts of service), or even just goes in for hugs on the regular (physical touch), these may be pure, simple signs of genuine interest. There are voices everywhere shouting at us about what we should make of a guy's behavior, but I want you to be willing to give good guys the benefit of the doubt. The dating game is tough on both sides, and you owe it to yourself to stay open enough to see what's possible.

So go ahead! Give a gift. Accept a gift. You never know how that gift might keep on giving.

CHAPTER 5

FIND A MAN WHO BRINGS YOUR MOM GIFTS

. . . and added, "He gave me these six measures of barley, saying, 'Don't go back to your mother-in-law empty-handed.'"

RUTH 3:17

If you find a man who is mindful of your mom, date him.

Why?

If he loves your mom, it is highly probable that he will get along with your friends, celebrate when you nurture friendships, and extend grace for family gatherings.

If a man honors the older generation, it is a good indicator that he will honor you. Take a look at the way he treats his mother. If he is impatient, coarse, and stingy, he will most likely treat you the same way.

Boaz wasn't dumb. He not only gave Ruth a gift, but he gave a gift to his future mother-in-law, too. Smart move, Bo!

CHAPTER 6

BOAZ OVER BROKEAZZ

Now Naomi had a relative on her husband's side,
a man of standing from the clan of Elimelek, whose
name was Boaz.

RUTH 2:1

Listen, homegirl. I don't want to come across as disparaging or demoralizing toward men. I love men the way Oprah loves bread. Whether it's my husband, father, brother, friend, or coworker, the men in my life are worthy of my affection and attention because I sincerely love them.

But some men should be classified as undatable. When searching for a potential date, don't be afraid of assessing their VDQ. *What is VDQ*, you ask? Let me educate you! VDQ stands for **Viable Dating Quotient**. If you are single or know someone who is single, make sure you do the homework before jumping into a relationship with someone who has a low credit score or, worse, a low VDQ.

Let's make a basic VDQ assessment:

VDQ Question 1: Does he love Jesus?

I don't care if your date has a ten-pound Bible buried somewhere in his closet and knows John 3:16. I'm asking you to seriously assess if he is passionate about God.

Someone hand me a praise hanky, because I'm about to PREEEEACH! If he isn't passionate about God, be prepared to date someone who will struggle with honoring sexual boundaries, resolving conflict, and self-sacrifice. How do I know this? Because these things are difficult for God-fearing Christians, so just know it's worse *without* the Spirit of God in a person to help set them straight.

If the answer to question 1 is yes, proceed to question 2.

VDQ Question 2: Does he have a job?

This is not vanity; this is responsibility. If a man wants to show maturity and availability, that starts with earning a living and being responsible enough to show up to work.

Living off welfare or a parent's trust fund is an indication that your dude isn't in a position to invest in you or a relationship. If you're reading this book and thinking, *This is so rude. I don't need someone to take care of me because I'm an independent woman who doesn't need to be won over by money*, let me first congratulate you on being a boss! But let me also warn you that if a man lives with his mother, who takes care of him and her eighty-five cats, he will certainly expect you to treat him the same way. Your independence can lead to his codependence.

Is there grace for a career transition or a loss of job? Absolutely. But if your potential Prince Charming lacks the motivation and sense of responsibility that pushes him to work, he might not be in a position to enter into an equitable relationship.

Let me also note that I'm not being greedy here. A job is a

job. This has less to do with the amount of money someone is bringing home and more to do with a person's work ethic and sense of obligation. Whether your guy works in a warehouse or the White House, this is about dedication and responsibility.

If the answer to question 1 and question 2 is yes, proceed to question 3.

VDQ Question 3: Is he friends with a bar of soap and a toothbrush?

(Note: Let me preface this last point with the understanding that this is my own personal preference. You are allowed to insert your own non-negotiables here [e.g., good with kids, must have a sense of humor, lives generously], but this is the third and final requirement I set for myself when I was dating. You can borrow it if you would like!)

Halitosis from hell is a sure sign a brother might be toothless by the age of fifty. If you want your significant other to have teeth throughout adulthood, ensure he is flossing, brushing, and rinsing on the regular.

If someone smells ripe on a date, first make sure it's not you. You're welcome. Then assess if his pungent body odor is something you find attractive or repellent. If you notice a lack of hygiene during the dating period, it will definitely be magnified the more comfortable you become in the relationship.

If your dating candidate didn't earn a perfect score, I would strongly caution you against moving forward. (The quotient we're after is THREE, not three hundred. Don't think this is a tall order. In fact, the bar is set low.) You could add your own questions to my VDQ evaluation, but I would suggest you not get carried away with overly specific, superficial qualities. Don't rule someone out before you've given him a chance.

I love using Boaz as a barometer for the type of person my

single friends should date because we don't know what he looked like, we don't know how old he was when he met Ruth, and we don't know how much money he had. Ruth may not have known much about him, but let's see what she *did* know about him and thereby learn what to look for in a potential date.

> Now Naomi had a relative on her husband's side, a man of standing from the clan of Elimelek, whose name was Boaz. (Ruth 2:1)

- **RUTH KNEW SOMEONE WHO KNEW HIM.** In dating situations, you might not always know someone before you go on a date with him. However, it's way less risky if a person you know can vouch for your potential date. Naomi, as we discover in later verses, knew exactly who Boaz was and encouraged her widowed daughter-in-law to pursue him.
- **BOAZ WAS A MAN OF STANDING.** In other words, HE HAD A JOB. His name wasn't Brokeazz, it was Boaz. As a business owner and landowner, this man was fiscally responsible and socially influential. I want my single sisters to find a man of good standing!
- **HIS NAME WAS BOAZ.** In addition to its meanings of "honor" and "integrity," the name *Boaz* could also be interpreted as "strength." Illustratively, his name also appears on one of the pillars of Solomon's temple.[1] Boaz was like a pillar of strength to hold up Ruth and Naomi so their lives wouldn't crumble. Find an emotionally and spiritually strong man to lift you up and empower you to be the woman God has called you to be.

Boaz continually displayed impeccable character, blessing everyone in the story. Many have called him a type of Jesus. And Jesus, as the great Charles Spurgeon said, is "our glorious Boaz."[2]

He is our Redeemer, our Savior, who took us in not because He had to, but because He **wanted** to.

You don't need a man to save you—you have Jesus for that. But Christlike qualities in a man you're dating are indications that you are pursuing your relationships wisely.

Ruthless

This might feel ruthless, but I believe we can handle the truth.

What would *you* score on the VDQ?

It's so easy to look at someone else and find fault with them. But we must also take time to be honest about where we are in life.

VDQ Question 1: Do you love Jesus?

Going to church once a month and listening to Hillsong United during your cardio sessions doesn't make you a lover of Christ. I'm talking about developing a relationship with the only One who truly knows you.

If you don't have a personal relationship with Jesus, no amount of love from a man will make you feel completely secure. If you don't love Jesus, there is no way you'll love yourself as He does, let alone love your significant other.

VDQ Question 2: Do you have a job?

For my single sisters out there: don't wait for a sugar daddy to cancel out your debt and make you a Real Housewife. Be a grown, independent woman who doesn't need someone else to meet her basic needs or validate her existence. Be responsible and take initiative to get your life together.

Unlike the Disney fairytale princesses many of us were raised idolizing, the women of the Bible worked. Ruth was in the fields gleaning, Rebekah tended the cattle, the Proverbs 31 woman was a merchant, and Lydia was a business owner. These women were esteemed, not for who they married, but for who they chose to be and how tirelessly they worked.

We are not desperate, dateless damsels waiting to be chosen. We are warriors who go to battle with the breastplate of faith like Deborah;[3] we are peacemakers who wear crowns to use our influence like Esther;[4] we are prophets who steward anointing to speak on behalf of God like Huldah.[5]

Get a job. Go to work.

VDQ Question 3: Are you friends with a bar of soap and a toothbrush?

Do you smell? More importantly, do you *know* if you smell? Be brave and ask a close friend for honest feedback on your breath and body scent. To paraphrase the Beatles, we get by with a little help from our friends!

Perfume and body spray only blend in with your natural body scent, so make sure you shower regularly and don't be afraid of a splash of perfume to help your natural scent.

A mentor once told me, "The only things a woman takes with her to her grave are her teeth and her wedding ring. So make sure you take care of both of them!" Don't demand a perfect Colgate smile from your date if your own gums are inflamed and you haven't flossed since high school.

If the answer to all three of these questions is yes, congrats! You have passed the VDQ with flying colors.

CHAPTER 7

SAY WHAT YOU WANT AND MEAN WHAT YOU SAY

*"Spread the corner of your garment over me, since
you are a guardian-redeemer of our family."*
RUTH 3:9

When I'm discussing relationships with men, I'm consistently asked, "What in the world do women want?" It doesn't offend me, because I totally understand this question. Women can send mixed signals. Women are intuitive creatures, inspecting other people's actions, words, body language, and intentions, but we can also make emotional decisions based on snap judgments. Basically, we care about *who* is saying *what* and *how*. But think about it, how many times have any of the following thoughts crossed your mind?

A guy you're attracted to gives you some attention, and
you consider him flirtatious and interested.
A guy who's not your type gives you similar attention, and
you decide he's clingy and needy.

A guy is intentional and direct, and you freak out that he's too forward and moving too fast.

A guy takes things slowly, and you wonder what his problem is.

A guy pays for dinner, and you think he's kind and caring.

A guy doesn't pay for dinner, and you assume he's only after one thing.

Sometimes women make it really hard for men. We say one thing and mean another.

For example:

Women: Do whatever you want.

Translation: *I'm not going to tell you if I think it's okay or not. You should know me enough by now to know if I'm okay with it. Which, by the way, I'm not. If you do this, we are through.*

Women: I need space.

Translation: *We are about to break up.*

Women: I'll be ready soon!

Translation: *I'll be ready when I'm ready. Could be ten minutes, could be an hour. Find something else to do.*

Women: We need to talk.

Translation: *I'm going to talk, you're going to listen.*

Women: Nothing's wrong.

Translation: *Did you seriously ask me, "What's wrong?" As if you don't know. Everything is wrong. Everything! Be afraid. Be very afraid.*

Women: Whatever.

Translation: *You have won this round, but I refuse to concede, so I'm dismissing that last point you made, and we shall never speak of this again.*

Women: Maybe.

Translation: *No.*
Women: We'll see.
Translation: *No.*
Women: Yes.
Translation: *Yes. Or maybe. But probably no.*

I understand that these might feel like gross generalizations or stereotypes, but may I remind you that stereotypes are based on a preponderance of truth?

In John Gray's bestselling book, *Men Are from Mars, Women Are from Venus: A Practical Guide for Improving Communication and Getting What You Want in Your Relationships*, he outlines the underlying differences in communication styles between men and women (and suggests that we are so different in our approaches that we are from different planets!).[1] According to Gray, men and women have different needs, goals, and values in the way they communicate. Understanding these differences is key to creating and maintaining successful relationships by being aware of how the different genders communicate and adapting one's style accordingly.

The main differences Gray identifies between the communication styles of men and women are as follows: Men are goal-oriented; they define a sense of self by their ability to achieve results. Women, on the other hand, are relationship-oriented; they define a sense of self by their feelings and by the quality of their relationships.

Men and women also cope with stress differently; men cope by withdrawing themselves from difficult situations while women cope by reaching out and talking about the causes of their stress. Gray coined the phrase, "Men go to their caves and women talk," to describe this psychological difference.

This could be a better foundation from which to observe the communication style between Ruth and Boaz as they come to the end of harvest season. Let's set up the scene . . .

The harvest celebration had come to a close, and Boaz left the party to head to the threshing floor, where his barley was stored. According to biblical historians, robbers would steal grain from landowners after they'd reaped their harvests, and it was common for these landowners to sleep near their grain piles. Per the instructions of matchmaking Naomi, Ruth did everything her mother-in-law told her to:

> "Now Boaz, with whose women you have worked, is a relative of ours. Tonight he will be winnowing barley on the threshing floor . . . . When he lies down, note the place where he is lying. Then go and uncover his feet and lie down. He will tell you what to do." (Ruth 3:2, 4)

(I want to pause for a second and highlight some truths before we progress in this story. This narrative is descriptive, not *prescriptive*. Meaning, the author is describing what happened, not prescribing that we follow suit. Times have changed, girlfriend! Don't go stalk a brother, lie at his feet, and blame me, Mama Naomi, or this book. Your actions are on you.)

Naomi sensed that it was high time Ruth made her desires known to Boaz. In Ruth 3:7, we see our heroine, as directed, quietly approaching her wannabe boo, Boaz. She uncovered his feet, lay down beside him, and was trying to fall asleep when something awakened Boaz in the middle of the night. Startled and shocked to see a woman lying at his feet, he asked, "Who are you?"

Side note on Boaz: he was a GOOD man. Instead of making a smooth move on a lovely lady lying languidly at his feet, he asked a question: "Who are you?" (Ruth 3:9). Why is this important? Because during this time, it was common for prostitutes to sell themselves on the threshing floor (Hosea 9:1). Boaz—whose name means honor and integrity (more on this in chapter 8)—didn't take advantage of the situation.

Ruth was obedient to her mother-in-law's wisdom, but notice there was no script to follow, no directions on what to do next. Naomi had gotten her beloved Ruth this far, and now it was time for Ruth to woman up! She was going to tell Boaz exactly what she wanted.

Wouldn't it be nice if we had permission to say what we wanted? **News flash: we do.** So many women struggle to vocalize their desires or even ask for clarity. It might come down to culture, history, psychology, or simple insecurity, but many of us have the propensity to shrink back and remain silent when what we crave are clear answers.

> We have permission to ask for what we want.

Especially when it comes to relationships.

Put yourself in Ruth's shoes. She was an infertile immigrant from a despised homeland who found favor with her boss. She was confused by Boaz because they sat together at lunch and he even gave gifts to her—*and her mother-in-law.* (Note: a man who gives food as a gift is a keeper!) But then, radio silence. They got along well, and she continued to work for him, but he made no move and never took the relationship further.

Have you been there? I have.

I met a guy at a church where I was volunteering. I referred to him as a unicorn, leprechaun, or *chupacabra,* because—like these mythical creatures—I wasn't sure men like him really existed. He was tall, athletic, educated, articulate, loved Jesus, flossed his teeth regularly, *and was single.* I mean, come on?! AND he was strikingly handsome! I almost left that out so I wouldn't sound too carnal, but this brother was fiiiiiiiiiine! Carry on.

I checked him out at church and online for a couple of months and discovered he was actually really normal. He loved his family, he loved ministry, he was goal-oriented, *and he was single.* We casually chatted at church, found ourselves on the same ministry team (it was coincidence, I swear!), and exchanged phone numbers. He called me about a project we were working on, and we spoke for over an hour. A few weeks later, he asked if I wanted to grab coffee after church.

The date was a ton of fun and lasted over two hours. When it was over, we hugged, and he said we should do it again. In my mind, this was going places! More coffee to be had! More dates to go on! More wedding venues to research! (Too far? I always take things too far.)

I would see him at church, and he'd give me a hug. He would see me walking down a hallway and wave. He would randomly text me that he was praying for me or send memes he thought were funny. He introduced me to his mom, who visited from out of town once. I saw these actions as little breadcrumbs I was sure were going to lead me to his heart. So I picked up the trail of crumbs (before I knew better than to settle for crumbs) and waited for him to make a move.

But this was basically the extent of our relationship for TWO YEARS. How do I know it was two years? Well, because I kept a journal entirely dedicated to him. I wish I was lying, but hand to heaven, I really did.

Do I sound crazy? Sure. But I really did think this was going places, so I prayed and journaled and journaled and prayed, and waited until the words in my journal and the prayer on my lips came to pass (and he became my hot husband and we did ministry together forever). THIS IS HOW EVERY GOOD CHRISTIAN WOMAN SHOULD ACT. Right? Ok, fine. The answer is a hard *no.* But nobody's perfect.

This might feel uncomfortable to discuss, so I will tread lightly. So many of my female friends sit around idly waiting and praying for God to shift someone's heart (Proverbs 21:1), but

Solomon wasn't writing about praying so hard that the heart of the single hottie you have been attracted to will change toward you. Do I believe it's okay to pray for doors to open to have a conversation with the person you're attracted to? Absolutely. Do I believe you have the power and authority to gain clarity and ask the nature of the relationship? Most definitely.

But I spent two years believing that this guy was "going to come around." After all, he was awesome, *I* was awesome, and we went on that one awesome date once upon a time ago. I honestly thought he was just taking it slow. I probably should've taken the hint (okay, *hintS*) that he wasn't interested, but I had this weird, hyperspiritual belief that I must *wait for the man to make the move and bring clarity to all things*. It seemed almost endearing to say that I was praying for God to change the heart of a man and give him eyes for me. But that is an outdated, patriarchal, and damaging current in the Christian river. We need to abandon ship.

Take some responsibility for your own situation. If what you need is clarity, you have permission to ask questions and express what you want in a relationship. Instead of wasting two valuable years of emotional energy, I could've easily (and casually) asked my former future husband if he saw us as just friends or more than that. There is nothing wrong in asking for clarity in relationships. Not only would it have saved our friendship, it would've saved me from a massive heartbreak.

There is nothing wrong in asking for clarity in relationships.

After waiting for this guy to ask me out again for two years, I saw him walk into church with a beautiful blonde whom he introduced to everyone as his FIANCÉE. Yes, I said fiancée. Imagine the hurt I might have saved myself if I'd only known to take a page from Ruth's playbook.

Ruth (aided by her matchmaking *yenta*) was smart. She was direct. She was clear. There were no games to play, no ambiguous emojis to decipher, no atonal text messages to try to interpret. She was a woman who drew a line and asked for what she wanted.

"Spread the corner of your garment over me, since you are a guardian-redeemer of our family." (Ruth 3:9)

Now, before you think Ruth asked for Boaz's coat because she was cold, understand that there was something huge going on here. Ruth's phrase was an idiom for "marry me." The gesture of a man covering a woman with his garment was a symbolic act, a declaration of a husband providing for his future wife (check out Ezekiel 16:8 for more on this). Ruth was clear in telling Boaz she wanted to be his wife!

Just retelling this story, I'm standing on my feet giving this woman a slow clap. She had *chutzpa*! You know what really happened on the threshing-room floor? Ruth had a DTR! Yup, a Defining-The-Relationship talk. You heard me right! She drew the line. She let him know what she wanted. In addition to letting Boaz know she wanted their relationship to turn into marriage, she also challenged him to back up his words. Look how smartly she did it:

The first time Boaz and Ruth had a conversation, Boaz affirmed her and acknowledged all the sacrifices she had made on behalf of her family. He also prayed that Ruth would "be richly rewarded by the LORD, the God of Israel, under whose wings [she was] to take refuge" (2:12).

If you get into the minutiae of the text, Ruth essentially asked Boaz to answer the prayer *he* prayed for her. Boaz asked God for a wing to provide shelter for Ruth. Ruth asked Boaz to *be* that shelter by marrying her.

Not only is this uncommon for women today, it would've been unheard of for women to be this forward during Ruth's time! And yet strong, bold Ruth allowed herself to be vulnerable and willing to be heartbroken for the sake of love and marriage.

This might feel like a stretch for some and a sigh of relief for others. To make sure we know how to have a DTR, here are some guidelines.

When to Have a DTR

At what point do you define the relationship? If you wait too long, you waste your time. If you move too soon, you run the risk of (1) making a hasty decision and (2) looking desperate or awkward (or both). Here are a few signs that warrant a DTR:

- If a guy has been texting or direct messaging you repeatedly, it's safe to assume he is at least interested in getting to know you.
- If a guy calls to check in or touch base a couple of times a week, that might be a sign he is attracted to you and cares about you.
- If a guy has asked you out several times and the dates have been fun and easygoing, he probably likes being around you.

If you are fine with generically communicating with someone as a means to get to know them, wonderful! But if you are questioning if this is more than a mere friendship, you have the grounds to casually, and without pressure, ask what's going on. Is this a friendship? Is this more than a friendship?

How to Have a DTR

Please note: having a conversation with anyone about where you stand in a relationship is hard. But if you value them and value yourself, be true and honest about your feelings. Here are a few tips:

- **BE CASUAL.** As Gray mentioned, if men sense high levels of emotion, they will retreat to a cave. Don't get crazy, don't cry, and don't look desperate. Act like a lady and handle yourself with class.
  - If you are having a DTR with someone you are *not* interested in, you might lead the conversation with, "Hey, I just wanted to tell you how much I enjoy our friendship. I love counting on you as my friend. Before any lines are crossed or communication is skewed, I just wanted to clarify that we are friends and I don't see us as anything more."
  - If you are having a DTR with someone you are interested in, you might lead the conversation with, "Hey, I love how much we get to hang out! It's always fun. But before I read into things or assume something that may not be real, I'm starting to develop feelings and don't want to be wrong. Are we just friends or do you see this turning into something more than friends?"

Both of these conversations are difficult to initiate, but when you own your feelings and ask for clarity, it forces the other person to own theirs.

- **BE CREATIVE.** If you don't feel brave enough to address the conversation head-on, be creative and find ways to get to the answer in less direct ways.
  - For example, use the excuse that your friends are always asking if there is something more going on. This way, you don't have to be the initiator per se. But I would

encourage you to make sure you leave the conversation with clarity and an understanding of where you stand in regard to a relationship.

- **BE MATURE.** If you are mature enough to bring up the conversation, you must be mature enough to handle the response.
  - If you find out someone isn't interested in you, be respectful of their feelings. It will probably hurt, but that isn't license to be spiteful, to plead, or to fly off the handle. You have full permission to stop the friendship if you need to. I would actually encourage that, so you don't waste time investing in a relationship you're more into than he is, but you don't have permission to be mean or rude. Act like an adult.
  - If you find out someone is interested in you, don't run off to start a mood board for your wedding on Pinterest. Be chill and see how things organically unfold.

How *Not* to Have a DTR

To ensure you jokers don't go rogue and act like darn fools, I'm also including some helpful hints about how **not** to have a relationship talk (learned firsthand by me or my friends). You're welcome in advance.

- **FIRST DATES.** If you are on your very first date with someone, don't try to define *anything*. I'm serious. Don't talk about defining politics, religion, or world crises. Ask questions and get to know what kind of person he is, but don't expect to have your future figured out by the time the check arrives. Use wisdom, friends.
- **TEXT MESSAGES.** Texting is a super great way to keep a relationship casual, make plans, or send awesome memes.

But please—for the sake of sanity—do **not** have a DTR via text message. Texting is not the way to have a mature, grown-up conversation. We can't read body cues, intonation, or inflection in text, so it's wiser to rely on good ol' face-to-face conversation.

- **ALCOHOL.** There is no such thing as "liquid courage." That is a lie. Alcohol will cloud your judgment as well as heighten emotions during difficult conversations. Put the booze down and be sober when talking to someone you care about. At the very least, you want to remember the conversation, right?!

Use your common sense, ladies! If you have known someone for one day, don't ask to start planning the wedding. If someone took you on a coffee date, don't discuss honeymoon destinations. If someone casually introduced you to a friend or family member, don't start naming your children. For the love of all things holy, be normal!

This might feel like too much for you to handle right now. It might feel too daring, too brave, or too embarrassing. But don't let social norms or insecurities keep you muzzled. There is nothing wrong with saying what you want.

Just ask my friend Cindy, who told a guy from work she was interested in him and wanted to get lunch together. She is now happily married (with two children) to a man who was so grateful she was brave enough to take the first step, because he wasn't, and he thought a woman like her would never go out with a guy like him.

Ruth knew what she wanted and wasn't afraid to ask it of Boaz. I pray you aren't afraid, either.

THOUGHTS FROM A THERAPIST

Dr. Deb on Rational Thinking

When it comes to communication and decision-making, the brain is wired to be both rational and emotional. Rational thinking involves facts, calculations, and tangible observations about the world around you. Emotional thinking is just like it sounds: reactions based on your current feelings. We tend to have a predominant type that we default to and that is enhanced when things like stress or conflict intensify our current circumstances.

While men and women have equal capacity for emotional and rational thought, the general tendency is for men to default to increased rational thinking and women to enhance their emotional mind-set when confronted with more complex decisions (like those involved in the initial stages of dating!).

Think of the last time you were interested in someone. No doubt your brain was flooded with emotional experiences—excitement, happiness, intrigue, a pinch of fear. As women, those emotions are our strength! They drive our actions, fuel our passions, and deepen our relationships. However, those emotions can also fog up the lenses of our present realities so our decision-making isn't as clearly discerning as we'd like it to be. How do you ensure your emotional filters aren't the overriding influence in your approach to relationship clarity? You **intentionally activate** rational thought to bring your brain back to balance.

In Bianca's example, emotions such as hope, longing, affection, and exhilaration were the influential factors in her decision to wait, at times painfully, for her unicorn to come around. Instead of letting your emotions *dictate* your decision-making, be intentional in using them to *discern* your decision-making. The experience of emotions such as hope, affection, and longing communicate that you are interested, that there is a desire to pursue something more than a casual friendship encounter. That's the discernment piece.

However, if you balance that with rational thinking based on observable facts (two years of occasional texts, random waves, and a church hug here and there), a more reasonable interpretation of the situation presents itself: *his* level of interest likely hasn't crossed the friend threshold. Still, do you know this for sure? No, not until you seek greater clarity by pursuing the conversation like Ruth did.

To do this, you can apply the same process of balancing emotional and rational thinking. The emotions associated with the vulnerable task of initiating a DTR can be intense. But observing the current dynamics of your interactions factually and without judgment can help you create a rational evaluation of the present reality. Here is some language to help you: "I am unclear on where we stand in the relationship, and clarity will help me discern how to proceed going forward." Intentionally allowing *both* rational thinking and emotional thinking to influence your decision-making increases the likelihood that you will engage in a more productive action that aligns with your core values and desires.

PART 2

Faith and Spirituality

If you are a Christian, you have probably been taught that faith plays a central role in your spiritual growth, maturity, and development. But unless we are taught what faith looks like on a practical level, our perception of spiritual growth might be confused. We may be pouring our efforts into behavior modification without real faith as the key to unlocking the life transformation our soul desires.

The challenge I'm observing among God's people is that faith, as a *concept*, is easy to talk about on Sunday at church, but we're not sure what faith looks like during the rest of the week.

Without an understanding of faith for practical, everyday living, we sometimes lay thin Christian platitudes over spiritual potholes of doubt with simple phrases like, "You just gotta have faith!" If we don't know how to apply faith in our daily lives, this can leave us feeling abandoned and confused when life's trials and questions come our way.

In the story of Ruth and Naomi, we see two women dealing with poverty, death, infertility, bitterness, isolation, and feeling abandoned by God—and that's just in the first two chapters of the book of Ruth! Needless to say, these women endured hardships like many of those we face today.

Using their life experiences as a grid for how faith and spirituality are formed, we will have conversations in this section about:

- Why our names and identities matter
- How to identify depression
- How to know God in times of affliction
- How God's loving-kindness—*hesed*—is with us even in loss
- Dealing with death
- What faith looks like in someone from a different background

These concepts are enormous, and discussing them can feel incredibly daunting, but each of the following chapters is aimed at simply opening up conversations. I'll provide lessons from women in my life and from our Hebrew heroines of yesteryear to help guide you toward a deeper understanding of all these concerns.

CHAPTER 8

WHAT'S IN A NAME?

*They married Moabite women, one named Orpah
and the other Ruth.*

RUTH 1:4

Unless you've legally changed your name, you've probably had no choice in the name people call you. I always think it's fun to sit with a pregnant woman and discuss possible names for her baby. Whether the names are inspired by a story or a family member, we intuitively know there is power in declaring and speaking destiny through the naming of a person.

I love discovering the meaning of my friends' names, but sometimes I'm stuck when I discover a friend's name is poorly chosen, sad, or, in some cases, downright offensive. Imagine my shock when I discovered my friend Kennedy's name means "deformed head," and Cameron's name means "crooked nose." My favorite character from Shakespeare's *The Merchant of Venice* was named Portia, and I loved it until I discovered it means "pig."

I'm obsessed with names and their meanings. Shakespeare famously asked in *Romeo and Juliet*, "What's in a name?" And though I don't believe a name should permanently define you, it does have the power to affect who you are.

I learned this from my mother, who painfully and laboriously chose names with purpose and meaning for all five of her children. My middle sister, Alexandria, embodies her name, as she is a "defender of mankind." My youngest sister was supposed to be born with terminal birth defects, and doctors encouraged my parents to abort her at six months in utero. She was born perfectly healthy, and Zoe Belle was named "beautiful God-given life" because that's exactly what she was. My name, Bianca, means "pure" or "white." My middle name means "flower" in Spanish (a name I proudly inherited from my Puerto Rican grandmother). Believing I would be a sweet aroma unto the Lord, my mother chose a name she thought reflected what I would become.

In Hebrew culture, a name was either a prophecy, foretelling some aspect of someone's life, or chosen to document the situation into which a person was born. The name Moses, for example, means "pulled from water," and our favorite floating freedom fighter was drawn, as an infant, out of the Nile. Jacob means "cheater," and as the Bible documents, this man was Shady McShade! So while we're on the topic, let's dig into the names in the Ruth narrative and discover *who* we are working with and *how* it can teach us about our lives.

The first name we see in the book of Ruth is Elimelek. His name means "my God is king," and his wife's name, Naomi, means "sweet" or "pleasant." Mrs. Sweety and Mr. My God Is King had two sons, whom they named Sick and Dying. I'm serious—the names Mahlon and Kilion literally mean "sick" and "dying"!

I know superstars are naming their children after herbs, fruits, and navigational directions these days, but nothing seems quite as foreboding as naming your sons Tuberculosis and Heart Disease.

We aren't told how, but Elimelek passed away. The irony is

that though his name meant "my God is king," he didn't trust his God to protect him, but instead left his homeland in an attempt to save his family from starvation on his own. And what happened? He died. Not only that, but as their names foretold, Mahlon and Kilion died, too. As a result, all three of their wives were widowed in Moab.

After the deaths of their husbands, Naomi and her two daughters-in-law, Ruth and Orpah, set off for Naomi's hometown of Bethlehem. On a hot, dusty desert road, Naomi stopped and told her sons' widows to go back to Moab—back to their families and their gods. She had nothing for them.

> Then Naomi said to her two daughters-in-law, "Go back, each of you, to your mother's home. May the LORD show you kindness, as you have shown kindness to your dead husbands and to me. May the LORD grant that each of you will find rest in the home of another husband." Then she kissed them goodbye and they wept aloud. (Ruth 1:8–9)

Through their tears, both women told Naomi they wouldn't leave her. But Naomi pushed back, telling them the reality was that all was lost. Orpah, whose name means "back of the neck," turned away and went back to Moab. But Ruth, whose name means "friendly companion," turned to Naomi and busted out one of history's greatest testaments to commitment, saying,

> "Where you go I will go, and where you stay I will stay. Your people will be my people and your God my God. Where you die I will die, and there I will be buried. May the LORD deal with me, be it ever so severely, if even death separates you and me." (Ruth 1:16–17)

Do you know what your name means? Do you know why you

were named what you were? Whether there is a personal story behind it or not, I believe we can reclaim our identities.

Know Your Name

In a large auditorium after a women's conference, ladies were filing out as music pumped energetically through the building. The excitement in the air struck a stark contrast with the words coming from Brianna's mouth. A new mother, she had stayed behind to talk to me, painfully unraveling the nightmare she was living. She was jobless, and her husband of five years had just deserted her and their newborn child to rekindle a relationship with an old flame. She held her baby tightly as she wept, and I wrapped my arms around her, listening as she whimpered, "I can't handle this. This is just too much."

In that moment, I was reminded of the definition of her name.

"Brianna, your name means 'strong'! You are strong and well able to handle this."

She looked at me, her expression serious. I thought I had offended her. Then she asked, "Why did you just say that?"

Embarrassed and caught off-guard, I stammered through my answer, explaining that *Brianna* is also my best friend's name and that's how I happened to know its meaning.

"I felt that you needed to be reminded that you embody strength, just like your name declares," I said.

"But how could you know that?" she persisted. "My mother used to tell me all the time that I was strong and able. She passed away a couple of years ago, but she always said she'd named me Brianna because I would need to be strong."

I smiled because I actually had no clue why I had said what I did. I could only surmise that God knew it was what Brianna needed to hear.

Sometimes we need a reminder of who we *are* in order to refute the lie of what we are *not*.

Maybe you've felt too weak to handle a challenge that sprung from nowhere and took you to your knees. Maybe you've failed at something and falsely believed that made *you* a failure. Worse yet, maybe you had ugly names spoken over you that negatively affected your identity. Were you called Fat? Did someone name you Stupid? Were you known as Slut?

As we head into Bethlehem through the pages of Ruth and Naomi's story, I want you to discover your name in the midst of whatever situation you're in. Not the name that was written on your birth certificate, but the name God whispered over you that same day:

Child of God.

No matter what names have been given TO you or spoken OVER you, nothing can replace or supersede your identity as HIS child. Child of God, your story is not done. Your parents may have given you a name, but your heavenly Father has given you your *identity*.

Renaming

The concept of *renaming* might sound foreign, but I believe our identities shift when our names do. For example, Jesus changed the name of Simon, one of his twelve disciples. Simon, which means "reed," became Peter, which means "rock" (see Matthew 16:18). Jesus said that on the confession of Peter, He would build His church. Peter had a shaky beginning but ended up being a mighty pillar of strength—a rock, if you will—in the early church.

If you love drama, then you'll love the dramatic story of Gideon, who was named Jerub-Baal by his father in Judges 6. Jerub-Baal means "contender with Baal" (the local god of the area).

But it wasn't until after an angel called Gideon a "mighty warrior" that his identity changed and his courage grew.

If names are important, renaming might be equally as important. It's interesting to note that both Ruth and Orpah are Hebrew names. Why is it interesting? Well, because they were Moabites. The names they were given at birth would have, in all likelihood, been in their native language, not in Hebrew.

Scholars and theologians believe Ruth's and Orpah's names were not their original or birth names, and that they were used in the biblical recounting of their story to reinforce the narrative. If the name Orpah means "back of the neck," was it an implication that Orpah turned her back on her friends? Scripture doesn't say as much, but the last Ruth and Naomi probably saw of Orpah was the back of her neck as she walked back to Moab.

And Ruth? Ruth means "friendly companion," and Ruth lived up to her new name as she remained with Naomi until redemption was found. Who wouldn't want a friend like Ruth?

In discovering that "Ruth" most likely wasn't Ruth's given name, we can take from this renaming that Ruth can be *anyone*. Any one of us can take her name! Instead of just *wanting* a friend like Ruth, we can *be* a friend like Ruth. We can choose to walk through life's trials and tribulations to find redemption together and in community, just like Ruth did for Naomi.

Names play a factor not only in *who* we are called to be, but in *how* we should live our lives. Whether you feel your given name is a perfect fit or couldn't be further from the mark, whether you've been called something awful by yourself or someone else, you can rename yourself and reclaim your identity.

Child of God, you are chosen, and you are His.

THOUGHTS FROM A THERAPIST

Dr. Deb on Identity

The concept of identity and our perspective of *self* comes through the cognitive process of thinking and reflection. Thoughts can be simply defined as ideas, opinions, and beliefs we have about the world around us, but also about ourselves and our identities. Thoughts can also have a powerful impact on our emotions and how we interpret them.

If we don't take time to consider the thoughts we have about *who* we are and *what* we are called to be—if we don't declare our identities—it's too easy to allow others to declare them for us. I've worked with clients who claim identities that other people have placed upon them. False identities such as "failure," "disappointment," or "not enough" mar our perceptions of our destinies and ourselves. When we make embracing our true identities as chosen children of God a daily discipline, the decisions we face and the interactions we have can be viewed through a clearer lens.

Let me give you an example. Let's say you failed miserably at a work project. Perhaps it wasn't your fault (you were given the responsibility, but perhaps you weren't given the authority to carry it out). Or, maybe it was your fault (laziness prevented you from finishing what you started). Regardless, you are feeling the overwhelming disappointment of failure. However, failure is not your name or your identity.

Choosing to believe in your true identity as a Chosen One of God allows you to experience failure as just that, a failure. It's a situational circumstance that brings feelings of discouragement, possibly anger or bitterness, maybe even inadequacy or fear of losing your job or the respect of your colleagues, but it is not WHO YOU ARE.

Allowing the thought that failure is *who I am* or *what I do* to invade your brain space can trigger powerful, challenging emotions that further influence our perceptions of self (*I feel like a failure* becomes *I am a failure*). If we are not careful, we can allow our issues to become our identities. You have the power to identify an emotion and yet not be *defined* by it.

- "I feel disappointed in this failure" (emotion).
- "However, I am a still a Chosen One" (name).
- "The core of who I am is not impacted by the circumstances and relationships around me" (identity).

CHAPTER 9

HAPPENSTANCE, COINCIDENCE, OR PROVIDENCE

. . . and she happened to come to the part of the field belonging to Boaz.

RUTH 2:3 ESV

In 2010, I sat in an arena in Atlanta with twelve thousand leaders from across the nation. People had flown in from all over the country to listen to leaders lead leaders. With all due respect to each of the people who spoke, I can't remember anything any of them said . . . except one.

The petite blonde with a blunt-cut bob wearing a black leather jacket practically floated onto the stage. Her Australian accent and high energy reminded me of a spiritual Crocodile Dundee—one who wrestled demons instead of crocodiles. Words were coming out of her mouth with such fury, it was like a fire I could feel all the way up in the venue's nosebleed seats where I sat. She spoke about the Good Samaritan, human trafficking, and leadership—all things I had heard about before—in a way I had never heard them. Everything around me disappeared.

After her session, it was time for the lunch break, but I couldn't eat. I was too struck by what I'd just heard. Something this woman said was now planted deep in my heart, but I had no idea what it would become. I just felt so lucky to have been there. *What a coincidence.*

A few months later, I was newly married and emceeing a conference in California, near my home. Part of my role at the conference was to interview the guest speakers from the main stage. When I received the list of people I would interview, I was shocked to see the name *Christine Caine* on my roster. The spiritual Crocodile Dundee from the conference in Atlanta would be speaking here in California—and I was going to interview her! *What a coincidence.*

My husband, who was starting an antitrafficking initiative at the church where he worked, found out that I was going to interview Christine and asked me to connect them. She is, after all, the founder of A21, a global antitrafficking organization. *What a coincidence.*

I was excited, but I couldn't articulate why. It wasn't simply because she had moved me with her powerful words a few months before. The expectation I felt was more of an internal faith that *something* was coming, *something* was on the horizon.

After the conference, Matt and I resumed life as normal. He stayed busy at his church in Irvine, and I continued working at my home church in Los Angeles, handling communications and marketing and commuting ninety minutes each way.

I had been part of my church from its inception, when my father started it twenty-seven years prior. To this day, it still feels like home. For years I volunteered in ministry there, worked in the office and built meaningful relationships that remain indelibly inked on my heart. But for everything The Ark in Montebello meant to my life, something was shifting in me.

I was good at my job and loved the people I worked with, but I ached for development and growth. Somewhere inside, I felt God telling me it was time to flourish in a new place. My life was changing and so was my calling. I needed to respond to the growing pull on my heart to step out in faith toward what God had planned for me—but I was afraid.

After I got married, I moved to Orange County, became a wife and a stepmom, and wanted to be fully integrated in their lives. But I still wanted to remain at my home church with my family and friends. In an emotionally gluttonous move, I wanted to have my cake and eat it, too.

I knew God was calling me to leave my proverbial nest and cling to this new life, but I fought it and made up every excuse I could think of.

How could I leave the comfort and familiarity of the place I called home?

How could I justify abandoning the people who relied on me?

How could Matt and I survive on only a single income?

I found myself crying in the bathroom nightly, feeling torn between where I was and where I believed God wanted me. Sobbing and spread thin, I prayed God would show me what He had for me while simultaneously asking that nothing change.

And then something changed.

I came home from work one night after my ninety-minute commute to find Matt in our small apartment kitchen. "What are you doing tomorrow night?" he asked casually as I greeted him with a hug and poured a glass of water. I said I was free and hoping to run some errands. In a cool and deliberately emotionless tone, he asked, "Do you want to have dinner with Nick and Christine Caine tomorrow night?" I slammed down my water glass on the counter and fired back, "IS THE POPE CATHOLIC? Are you kidding me? I'm dying! No, I'm dead. I'm talking from my grave. Oh my word. Yes, yes, YES. I would love to have dinner with them!"

My heart began racing. I knew this was the start of something enormous, but I still couldn't figure out what—or how any of it was even happening.

Matt explained that he and Christine had connected at the conference I'd emceed and had been in touch on and off since then. She and her husband happened to be in town the next day and wanted to have dinner. *What a coincidence.*

Next, I did a hundred cartwheels, shrieked like a twelve-year-old at a Taylor Swift concert, and danced the running man in my sock-clad feet. Then, after a volume-speaking eye roll from Matt, I quickly composed myself and promised to be on my very best behavior. The woman who had stirred my passion for social justice had invited us to dinner to discuss human trafficking at the precise time I was begging God to show me where to move next. It was utterly thrilling—and couldn't possibly just be coincidence.

Nothing Just Happens

The idiom *nothing just happens* is rooted in a biblical understanding that God is sovereign; He is in control of **all** things.

It's not happenstance.

It's not coincidence.

It's not chance.

It's *providence*.

Simply put, providence encompasses every aspect of the created order. From beginning to end, from heaven to earth, from animate to inanimate, from individuals to nations, from hours to ages, from weeds to wheat, from birth to death, from catastrophe to calm, nothing exists outside the loving presence and involvement of the heavenly Father. In His wisdom, power, righteousness, and love, He is working all things together for His own glory and for our eternal good.[1]

We can see providence in the life of Ruth, who found herself *coincidentally* working in the field of a single, successful distant relative.

Ruth had hit rock bottom. She was devastated by the loss of her husband, destitute, and displaced from the only home she'd ever known. But in a bold leap of faith, she followed the whisper in her heart and set off with Naomi toward Bethlehem. What reason could she have had to believe she'd be better off there? None but faith, friends. None but faith in God's providence.

> So she set out and went and gleaned in the field after the reapers, and she happened to come to the part of the field belonging to Boaz, who was of the clan of Elimelech. (Ruth 2:3 ESV)

I love the way the Scripture adds to the drama of this story! "She *happened* to come to the part of the field belonging to Boaz, who was of the clan of Elimelech." Nowhere else in the Old Testament is any event described with this phraseology. "She happened" is an ironic, tongue-in-cheek writing device the author of the book has employed to grab our attention. It's used to challenge us as readers to consider the reality that no part of Ruth's (or Naomi's) story was in any way, shape, or form the result of mere happenstance. It was purposeful. God was intimately involved and orchestrated every step.

Think about the story with an ironic tone in mind:

Ruth *happened* to abruptly move from Moab to Bethlehem.
She *happened* to be starving and sought work in a field.
Though the fields were all lined up next to one another, she
    happened to pick Boaz's field.
Boaz *happened* to be an honorable, eligible relative with a
    passion for God.
Ruth just *happened* to pick *that* field.

This isn't happenstance, coincidence, or chance. It's the *providence* of God, which is a central theme in the book of Ruth.

Sometimes God works visibly—the Red Sea will part, manna will fall from heaven, a burning bush will start talking. Other times, God works invisibly through providence—Ruth "coincidentally" found herself working in a field that "just so happened" to belong to Boaz.

As James says, every good and perfect gift comes from God.[2] Isaiah 65:11 rebukes those who believe in random timing or good fortune. Our good and gracious Father makes a way when there is no way, and what others may chalk up to chance, *we* know to be the divine providence of our sovereign God. And how heartening to recognize that our lives aren't *up* to happenstance or some finicky Lady Luck. God's got us! We need only to step forward in faith, knowing He's ordering those very steps toward what is ultimately best for us.

It Just So Happens

Over dinner, Christine and I hit it off. Through cackling laughter and our definitely-too-loud-for-an-Orange-County-restaurant conversation, we got to learn more about what we each felt called to do. You can't take a passionate Greek Australian and a mouthy MexiRican and expect us to keep quiet for long. (Sorry, Matt!) Christine explained the global work she was doing with A21, the organization she founded to combat human trafficking. When she asked what I did, I shared my background in marketing and communication, and my passion for storytelling. I hadn't foreseen the conversation taking this shape, but our dinner was going better than I had dreamed!

We hadn't even finished our appetizers when Christine leaned back in her chair and brazenly asked, "So . . . what are you doing with your life?" My heart pounded, my stomach dropped, and I paused, blinking. I wanted to rattle off long lists of ministries I'd led, brag on my graduate degree, and gush over my brand-new marriage to a visionary missions pastor. These things were impressive, right? But I knew that, deep inside, as wonderful as they all were, if I mentioned them now, they would only be smoke and mirrors, aimed at projecting success and hiding from what I believed God was calling me to.

Should I say what was still unclear to me, but I believed to be true? Could I confess to a near stranger what purpose and calling were starting to look like to me?

I took a long sip of water and swallowed it slowly (my foolproof stall tactic). A gentle breeze blew through the patio where we were seated, and I felt like I was having an Acts 2 moment; this was my Pentecost. In a split second, I decided I would finally express verbally what God had whispered to me internally. I brimmed with certainty. The heavens would open, the spirit of God would descend on me like a dove, and the angels would erupt in joyous chorus because I had found my PURPOSE!

"I want to use words as weapons and give them to people who need to learn how to fight for who they are. I want to turn the world upside down—or right-side up—like Jesus," I said.

Christine's response was quick and flat. "Are you doing that writing your *blog*?" she asked.

I clutched my proverbial pearls. There were no doves, there was no Pentecost wind blowing, and any enthusiasm surrounding my brave declaration was immediately gone. Exposed and unsure of how to respond, I stammered back: "I think so?"

I was terrified. *Was I making a difference? Was I where I was supposed to be?* I believed God had called me to storytelling, to use my words and theology to fight for freedom. I had faith—even in my fear—God would show Himself as faithful. All I knew how to do was to get up, show up, and never give up. God would providentially put me where I was supposed to be.

I might've been unsure of my efficacy, but I was sure about *not* arguing with Christine. Arguing with this passionate woman would be pointless because (1) she's Greek (you will always lose), and (2) she was right. With gifts and talents and words inside of me, I knew I was supposed to do something specific; I just didn't know *what* it was. Unless you know *what* God is calling you to say, it doesn't matter *how* you say it. God will reveal what to say, how to say it, and, equally as important, when to say it.

And that's when it happened. Christine and Nick offered me a job at A21 overseeing social media, branding, and communication. With time, I would grow there, and become the organization's Chief Storyteller, receiving the honor and privilege of communicating the stories of the voiceless.

It *just so happened* A21 was looking for someone to oversee digital marketing.
And it *just so happened* that this was my skill set.
And it *just so happened* I wanted my words to be weapons.
And it *just so happened* I would have the opportunity to use them to arm resilient survivors of human trafficking all over the world.

God placed me at a conference in Georgia months before it would lead to a major life change and a job I'd thrive in for years. He'd been moving in my husband's ministry to align Matt's work with Christine's long before we sat down for our first interview. He'd cleared my busy schedule to free me up for the one dinner conversation that would change the entire course of my career and lead me (through many twists and turns) to the desk from which I'm typing this very book.

I couldn't see any of that from the teary puddle on my bathroom floor. I was terrified of change and nearly immobilized by uncertainty. But my faith kept bringing me back to the promise of God's providence, and in His time, I saw it all work together for good.

In moments when you question why you are where you are, just know that nothing is without reason. When you least expect it, when you feel out of place and out of sorts, when you are surrounded by twelve thousand leaders and you are a nameless face in a large auditorium, know that God is at work. He sees the moments when you cry out and He *just so happens* to *coincidentally* place you in the field where you'll find your harvest. Friends, that's not happenstance—it's providence.

THOUGHTS FROM A THERAPIST

Dr. Deb on Anxiety

Deeply rooted in fear, anxiety often results from experiencing overwhelming emotions related to the unknown. *How will I navigate this? How will I overcome this? How will I survive?* The greatest counseling truth I can give my clients is to confidently hold to the truth that God is purposefully orchestrating each part of our journeys. There is no happenstance. The event you're navigating, no matter how big or how small, will lead to another part of God's plan for your life.

I believe Ruth faced anxiety. She most likely felt overwhelming emotion when it came to the mental and spiritual health of Naomi and the basic daily need for shelter and food. With stress this high, Ruth was undoubtedly facing emotional turmoil. Nevertheless she persisted—she took a new step every day.

In the middle of feeling completely alone and unsure, trust God as your provider. Knowing that there is no chance of happenstance in His narrative will provide just enough comfort in the midst of anxiety and fear to take another baby step forward. But we must move forward, or anxiety will keep us stuck.

CHAPTER 10

THE INSIDE OUTSIDER

*At this, she bowed down with her face to the
ground. She asked him, "Why have I found
such favor in your eyes that you notice me—a
foreigner?"*

RUTH 2:10

Amina slipped into the sanctuary wearing a Middle Eastern head
wrap and holding an Arabic Bible. She stood out among the blonde,
fair-skinned women I usually saw at our the church we attended
on Sunday mornings. As someone who loves people-watching and
imagining the stories of strangers' lives, I was intrigued. All by herself, she sat patiently waiting for the service to start.

As the congregation began to file in, greetings were exchanged
between friends, and seats which had been saved with handbags
and sweaters were emptied in order to welcome family members.
But Amina remained alone, sandwiched between two empty
chairs. She was isolated—in the center of our community. I
watched this fascinating stranger as she sang every lyric to every
song, seemingly content to worship in solitude.

In all fairness, I don't think anyone maliciously or deliberately chose not to sit next to Amina. At least, I hope not. And I can't blame anyone for not engaging with her because I didn't, either. But as I watched her, it pained me to see everyone treat her almost as if she weren't there.

As a sidebar, I'm a Christian who loves church, but I've always loathed that moment during the service when the pastor or worship leaders said, "Now turn to your neighbor and greet them!" Is there anything worse than feeling obligated to shake hands with people you've never met and exchange mandatory small talk? I always felt there was something inauthentic about this exchange. It made me squirm. But on this Sunday, my mind shifted a bit. I decided that if what I called "forced fellowship time" felt insincere, it was because I was insincere.

"Good morning," I said cheerfully as I bounded across the aisle to introduce myself to the woman I'd been watching. Her large, dark eyes met mine with an almost imperceptible sigh of relief. She smiled and said hello, but then, as if she assumed our conversation was done, she sat down. On any other Sunday, I would've been happy to have done the same. However, this newer, smarter, better version of Bianca was sincere and authentic and really cared about "fellowshiping" with my neighbor. Especially a neighbor I didn't see being welcomed by anyone else.

"I'm Bianca," I said. "Is this your first time here?"

She shook her head no.

"I've been coming here for three weeks, but I don't really know anyone. My name is Amina." She blushed, looking down at her folded hands, and then blurted out, "I'm from Syria. Sorry my English is so bad."

It was the first time I had seen her on campus, but I hoped it would not be the last.

Months earlier, the church we attended had hosted a panel on immigration and the church's responsibility to those seeking asylum. There were advocates, lawyers, and community pastors who debated and discussed the future of American immigration. The event was covered by the local newspaper, and response in the community was intensely divided, to say the least. The church was trying to facilitate an open dialogue about the Christian response to immigration, but it was painful to see our community polarized by the apparent fear of foreigners moving in and taking over. I'm a first-generation American, the daughter of a Mexican immigrant, and I understand personally the longing of those who risk their very lives to pursue their dreams in the Land of the Free.

I didn't know Amina's story, but I recognized the look on her face—the look of exclusion, the empty ache of longing to belong. I recognized it because I've worn the same look. I understood it because I've felt the same thing.

From the beginning of time, people have experienced the sting of separation and the pain of feeling unseen. For much of my time in college, I struggled to find a way to feel like I belonged in a very privileged, almost all-white student body. But it's not always a matter of color or class. Cain felt overlooked in his labors; Jacob was jealous of his father's favorite son, Esau; Joseph's brothers so longed for their father's attention they faked his death and sold him into slavery. Though our situations are extremely varied and our experiences aren't always the same, the Bible is full of characters who have felt what we have felt: excluded, unwanted, judged.

The beginning of the book of Ruth lays out all its characters. Sandwiched between verses is a small line we are prone to overlook: "They married Moabite women . . ." (Ruth 1:4). These words might not bear weight or context in our Western minds, but let's unravel what Ruth went through in regard to racism, prejudice, and feeling unwelcome.

Ruth was from Moab, which was roughly thirty miles from Bethlehem—a two-to-four-day walking journey. The history of the Moabites wasn't necessarily one to be proud of. The city was considered to be a godless place. Those who occupied Moab were descended from the child born out of incest between Lot and his own daughter. Throughout history, the Hebrews experienced ongoing hostility with the Moabites, in large part because the Moabites worshiped the false god, Chemosh.

Though it wasn't technically forbidden for the Hebrews to marry Moabites, it was definitely frowned upon. King David, in Psalm 60:8, wrote that to the Lord, "Moab [was] his washbasin." Being from Moab wouldn't have afforded a woman the kind of family heritage a Hebrew family would want to welcome.

But in spite of this, Naomi welcomed Ruth into her family, and Ruth chose to worship the one true God, Yahweh. When her husband died, Ruth was left with the option to return home or follow her Jewish mother-in-law. She was at a proverbial fork in the road: go back to Moab and the false god, Chemosh, or follow the Lord God of Israel. She chose the latter. On a hot desert road, en route to Bethlehem, Ruth confessed her desire for and belief in the one true God.

> But Ruth replied, "Don't urge me to leave you or to turn back from you. Where you go I will go, and where you stay I will stay. Your people will be my people and *your God my God.*" (Ruth 1:16, emphasis mine)

This was a bold move from Ruth. It wasn't simply that she chose to follow God and lived happily ever after. She headed to Bethlehem, where she would be a stranger in a strange land. She didn't have a Jewish husband, she didn't have any Jewish children, and she had no money. Basically, she had nothing to even remotely validate or justify her being there, among a people who historically despised her own. It's safe to assume she wasn't well-received.

Maybe when I saw Amina walking into church, I saw a little

of Ruth in her. Of course, I didn't assume she was widowed or broke or accustomed to idol worship, but I had been in that very same room just a few months earlier when members of my own community expressed the feeling that people like Amina simply didn't belong.

At the time we met, I didn't know she was a Syrian refugee. I didn't know she faced religious persecution for sharing her faith in Jesus with her community. I didn't know she read the article in the newspaper about our church's stance on immigration months before and how the congregation was split on how to respond. I didn't know she waited on the bus to get to church. And I didn't know she had been unwelcome at other churches she had visited. But when I heard Amina's story, it echoed Ruth's, and I was nothing short of astounded by the immensity of her faith.

Plenty of characters in the Bible are known for their faith. From Abraham to Moses to Mary and Joseph to the apostle Paul, the Old and New Testaments are filled with stories of people doing heroic deeds in the name of God. But Ruth's story is uniquely powerful.

Why?

Because *God never spoke to her.*

Ruth didn't hear a voice from the heavens like Abraham or encounter a burning bush like Moses. She didn't have a prophetic word like Deborah. She didn't get a sign like Gideon. She didn't get squat! But this despised, barren, widowed Moabite who once bowed to idols now found herself in a new land with new people and a new God. Did this stop her from dreaming? Did it stop her from working? Did it stop her from fighting for her life? No.

The same could be said for Amina. She fled Syria because of religious persecution; family members and friends were literally being killed for their faith. On arriving in America, Amina had no job, no home, no money, and no family. But she had her faith. I thought about how often I caught myself complaining about crowded church parking lots and annoying "forced fellowship" during Sunday services, and meanwhile, this woman had fled a country that kept her from openly worshiping God at all! Amina, like Ruth, worked hard to provide for herself and create a new life and family in the American church. And her journey wasn't easy.

Shameless stares and sideways glances reinforced the skepticism Amina felt when she walked into various churches in our area. Honoring her heritage by wearing her traditional head covering, she felt ostracized by the American church culture and struggled to find a church home that would welcome her.

You don't have to be an immigrant or hail from a Muslim country to feel like you've been on the outside looking in on the party. The feeling of exclusion is felt by all of us at one point or another:

The coworkers who all went to lunch without you
The conversation that halted when you walked over
The clique that excluded you
The friend who rejected you
The party you weren't invited to

We really can't control whether the people we encounter will understand or even care about our journeys. Chances are, there will always be places where we feel a bit like outsiders. There may be entire communities that seem to reject us. But as Ruth fought for her job, her family, and her name—and as Amina fought for her escape, her liberty, and her beliefs—I pray we learn from the faith of these women. I pray also that we see the struggle of these women, and in so doing recognize our own capacities to make them feel welcome.

In faith, Ruth found a new home in Bethlehem. In faith, Amina found a new home, too. Several weeks after we met, she attended a women's Bible study on campus and was welcomed by a group of women who opened their arms to her. The last time I saw her, Amina was surrounded by women who clucked around her like mother hens. We hugged, and she introduced me to the ladies she referred to as her moms. Mom Joan. Mom Helen. Mom Katherine. The moms had been introduced to Amina at their Bible study, and they each took initiative in helping her feel as though she belonged—not just in a new church but in a new country. They helped her with her résumé, took her to get her driver's license, and Mom Helen let Amina stay in her guest room to save money until she could move closer to church.

I smiled at Amina and said, "It looks like you are living the teenage American dream at the young age of thirty!"

She shook her head from side to side, and her head wrap swayed accordingly. "No," she said in improved English. "It's much better than the American dream. I'm living the God dream."

Be an Includer

What if we positioned ourselves to actively seek out those who are excluded? Instead of only wanting someone to fix our own story, why couldn't we play a part in redeeming someone else's?

Do for someone else what you wish was done for you. Invite the shy girl from your office out to lunch. Reach out to a friend who is isolated and depressed. Be intentional and introduce yourself to someone of a different ethnicity or nationality. Celebrate and welcome the outsider, the immigrant, the poor, and the marginalized. Need I remind you that Jesus, at one point or another, was labeled all of these, and it didn't stop Him from being an inviter?

In fact, He invited a fisherman, a doctor, a tax-collector, and an altogether motley crew of men to be in His circle. These outsiders became insiders and turned the world upside down. Imagine what you can do when you invite those whom no one else has chosen! You might just change the world.

THOUGHTS FROM A THERAPIST

Dr. Deb on Rejection

When it comes to experiencing rejection, psychologists have discovered that the same part of the brain that registers and reacts to physical pain is also activated when we encounter the emotional pain of feeling excluded.[1] The hurt you have when you feel left out registers in the same part of your brain as when you feel the physical hurt of stubbing your toe. Feeling like an outsider desperately looking in can be emotionally excruciating! Social psychologists have identified numerous consequences to feeling left out, including increased feelings of anger, anxiety, depression, and jealousy; reduced motivation; lack of self-control; difficulty sleeping; and lower self-esteem.[2]

Unfortunately, the same fear of rejection we feel based on how we've been treated by others is what can prevent us from reaching out to others who might also be experiencing the pain of exclusion. Thankfully, there's an antidote to feeling left out: create psychological safety.

Psychological safety refers to the security we need to feel confident in taking risks in our relationships with others.[3] It's like the emotional parachute we need before we'll even consider jumping out of the plane! When we feel psychologically safe, we're more likely to take chances because we have confidence in belonging to someone or something. However, it's all too easy to place responsibility for creating a sense of belonging on the people around us—developing expectations that others need to reach out to us instead of the other way around. But what if we could create our own sense of psychological safety to help propel us to reach out to the "outsider"? Creating a sense of belonging is as simple (and as complex!) as defining to whom and to what you belong.

Jesus reached out to the "least of these" because He knew His identity and belonging were rooted definitively in bearing the image of and being One with the Father. The beautiful thing is, we hold the juxtaposition of being both fellow image-bearers and fellow "least of these." We already have a place of belonging, and if we're willing to commit to a biblical understanding of this instead of an earthly one, we can create our own psychological safety.

CHAPTER 11

KNOW WHAT YOU WANT

"I am your servant Ruth," she said. "Spread the
corner of your garment over me, since you are a
guardian-redeemer of our family."
RUTH 3:9

I sat at my desk overwhelmed by the tasks, deadlines, budgets, and emails piling up as every variety of reminder notice seemed to be popping on my laptop screen at once. My husband, Matt, and I were forty-nine days from launching our church, The Father's House Orange County, and everything seemed to be mounting, especially the bills. In a moment of absolute frustration, I dropped my forehead on my cluttered desktop and whispered, "I can't do this. I just can't do this anymore."

The weight of launching a church, raising a family, traveling for work, leading a nonprofit prison initiative, and writing my second book did, at times, feel like a burden. But it was a burden I could carry. The moment the bills started to come in, that burden turned into a boulder, one I was certain I couldn't even begin to lift.

Eyes closed, head down, I felt insecurity creep in and cause me to question everything. *Am I really called to this? Do Matt and I have what it takes? How will we raise the money we need?*

Suddenly the Old Testament character Gideon came to mind. If you're not familiar with this man, head to Judges 6 and check out his amazing story! Gideon wanted foolproof certainty that God expected him to lead the fight against the enemies of His people. He not once but *twice* asked for signs as proof of God's faithfulness. Then before subsequently leading him into a successful battle, our good God showed up and graciously gave Gideon everything he had asked for.

My mind wandered to the Gospels. Throughout these books, I recalled Jesus asking the sick, the blind, and the lame the same question: **What do you want me to do for you?** Of course Jesus already knew the needs of everyone He encountered, but He asked them to articulate their requests.

Suddenly I saw it differently. If God was going to move for me, I'd have to ask for exactly what I wanted!

This wasn't always easy for me. I remember hearing in Sunday school that it was selfish to ask for things that I wanted because there were so many kids around the world in need.

My little eight-year-old brain understood this message as "do not ask God for anything but absolute necessities," but as an adult, I am certain that God wants to both know deeply and shape properly the longings of our hearts. The question I have been forced to wrestle with is, *Do I even know what I want?* Sound familiar, friend? Do *you* know what you want?

Let's dig a little deeper there. Sometimes it feels selfish to ask for what you want. Like my Sunday school teacher said, "Needs are greater than wants." We must first distinguish between a desire that brings God glory and a desire that brings us glory. I have experienced firsthand what happens when our wants drive us to unhealthy places.

E.g., *ME*. If you ask me to make a list of the things I want, I would ashamedly admit that the list would include a mansion in

Newport Beach, a customized Bentley like Kim Kardashian's, and a yacht to rival Jay-Z's.

James 4:3 addresses this clearly: "When you ask, you do not receive, because you ask with wrong motives, that you may spend what you get on your pleasures." And brother James is right! So we shame and beat ourselves and think of all the sad little children in the world that don't have anything. We stop asking because we ask with wrong motives.

Buuuuuuut (and it's a big but), we completely ignore the previous wisdom in the verse before: "You do not have because you do not ask God" (James 4:2). Wrong motives are, well, *wrong*, but they are the secondary issue. The primary issue is that we've stopped asking. *If you are not asking for the right things, it's because you don't know what you want.*

If you don't know what you want, there's no way you can ask for it. More importantly, *if you don't know what you want, you're going to get what you* don't *want.*

This concept might feel vague or maybe even entirely new to you, but let's make it as simple as possible. Why not start by asking God to put HIS desires in your heart? Ask God to form and mold your heart to be in alignment with His. Can you imagine what would happen if God's will and our desires aligned harmoniously? We'd walk in the fullness of our calling and witness God do the impossible through *us*!

Ask Not, Have Not

Nearly ready to throw in the towel, I reread Gideon's story and was inspired by his brazen faith. I pulled out my journal and felt moved to ask God for ten thousand dollars to help launch our church. And not just ten thousand dollars, but ten thousand dollars in the span of seven days. I was confident that God was going to see the work we were doing and give us what we needed to move on and advance the gospel. More Bibles in prison! More people coming to church! More lost souls finding Jesus! Of course God was going to answer my petition!

For the next seven days, I set out to pray this miracle in. I was serious! I'm talking Old Testament – level serious. As in, I copied the ancient prophet Daniel and prayed about it morning, noon, and night. On my knees, forehead pressed to the ground, I pleaded that God would open the heavens and give us the precise amount of money that we needed to reach a big goal.

Every day I checked the mailbox because I believed God was going to send us the money. Every day I checked my bank account in case God direct-deposited the funds straight from heaven. Every day I texted Matt to see if someone had made a surprising donation. Nothing.

As my weeklong prayer party came to an end, I confidently placed my head on my pillow and smiled because I *knew* God was going to answer my prayer by the time I opened my eyes the next morning! But when I woke, I realized that the week was over and we still had mounting bills, church needs, and work deadlines. *What happened? Was God even listening?*

Confidently Courageous

In Ruth 3, Naomi gave Ruth specific instructions to connect with Boaz, their family member who could redeem them. This was their last chance at survival. However, pay attention to the small fact that Naomi did not tell Ruth *what to say*. When Ruth had followed instructions and came face-to-face with Boaz, it was up to her to ask for what she wanted:

"Who are you?" he asked. "I am your servant Ruth," she said.
"Spread the corner of your garment over me, since you are a guardian-redeemer of our family." (Ruth 3:9)

Ruth knew what she wanted and wasn't afraid to ask for it. (Well, maybe she was afraid. Who wouldn't be afraid to ask outright for a marriage proposal? But she asked for it anyway, which made her even braver!)

Like Gideon, Ruth articulated what she wanted. And to be clear, what she said in modern terms was this: claim me as your wife, as is your duty.

I think many of us don't ask for what we want because we are afraid we will be let down. Maybe we want to protect God's reputation, not embarrass Him if He doesn't come through, so we pray small prayers and ask for small things.

Ruth's request was honored. In a beautiful example of personal desire and God's will coming together, Ruth demonstrated how to seek wisdom from others and bravely ask for what she wanted. She was confidently courageous in claiming her rightful spot within Boaz's household, and I want us to live the same way.

Divine Time

I became very emotional in the days that followed my week of prayer. To be clear, we had been praying about our church plant for months—it was only in the week I just described that my prayer took this particular shape. I questioned my calling and questioned if God even cared about all we were sacrificing. Through it all, I pushed forward and *chose* to believe God was with us, even if we still had thousands of dollars to fundraise.

Three weeks later I flew to London to speak at a women's conference. I opened the event on a Saturday morning, preaching like my life depended on it. I shared the vision for our church plant and how I believed God had called us to three tens: ten churches in ten years reaching ten thousand people. While I'm not sure the proper English crowd knew quite what to do with me, they were incredibly gracious and stood in faith for our vision.

I wasn't expecting what came next. The speaker who followed me was an African American pastor from Los Angeles, California, only forty minutes from where I lived. He took the stage, made a beeline to the podium, and declared, "Bianca, I believe so firmly in the vision that God has given you and your husband that we want to add one more ten to your vision. Our church is going to give you ten thousand dollars to help with your church plant."

The auditorium erupted in applause. I wanted to cry—okay, okay, I *did* cry! But I wasn't just crying over the generous gift. I was crying because God faithfully answered my prayer after all.

Ten thousand dollars.

God Almighty took me to a conference all the way across the globe to meet a pastor who lived forty minutes from us who was going to rally his church in answer to my prayer with a donation of *exactly* ten thousand dollars. There is nothing else to call that but providence!

I boldly asked. God delivered. Can I get an amen?

Greater yet, and the cause of even more tears, was the realization that it was never about the money. The donation was a game changer, but we still had lots of bills to pay. That pastor's gift was a sign that God was with us, for us, and covering us, just as Boaz covered Ruth. We simply needed to ask Him for what we needed. Then, when we'd fully surrendered to our dependence on Him, in His perfect timing (not mine), God answered our prayer, and it was celebrated by many!

We don't need to protect God's ability or capability by praying small prayers. God is trying to break out of your small dreams, your small asks, and your small desires and pull you up to His big dreams, His big plans, and His big desires.

Our Great Boaz

Charles Spurgeon, preacher and pioneer of faith in the nineteenth century, referenced Jesus as our "great and glorious Boaz" because as Boaz redeemed Ruth, Jesus has redeemed us. Let's follow in Ruth's footsteps and become courageous in voicing our desires.

- **IF YOU WANT GOD TO MOVE FOR YOU, MOVE TOWARD GOD.** Just as Ruth boldly and bravely lay at the feet of Boaz, we, too, must have the confidence to approach Jesus and tell Him what we want. We can initiate intimacy by drawing near to Jesus, the way Ruth drew near to Boaz. It can be uncomfortable and require boldness, yes? Yes. But the rewards are well worth it.
- **IF YOU WANT GOD TO MOVE, DELIGHT IN HIM NO MATTER THE OUTCOME.** Psalm 37:4 says, "Take delight in the LORD, and He will give you the desires of your heart." When you fall in love with God, He places desire in your soul and passion in your heart. I didn't dream about planting a church (quite the opposite!), but I did pray for years to discover how I can love God and others well. In this process, God shaped my heart, and I adored the people God was bringing to us looking for a community to call home. Their stories, their faces—it shaped my heart to see God in the middle of it all, and it aligned my heart to His. God shapes your future by shaping your heart. If what you want remains unclear, consider that you might not be letting God get close enough to shape your heart. God wants to shape what you want and give you what you long for. Ruth was infertile and a widow, yet she still chose to serve God. Ruth didn't have a home, husband, or child, but she found true love and acceptance amongst God's people. We, like Ruth, need to believe in His perfect timing and declare the words of Jesus before heading to the cross: ". . . yet not my will, but yours be done."[1]

Is there a desire buried deep inside your soul? Is there a dream burning in your spirit? Do you have a request so big that it almost dares you to step into the presence of God and ask with brazen hope and faithfulness?

God shapes your future by shaping your heart.

It is Jesus whispering to your soul the way He whispered to the blind, the lame, and the dying: *What do you want me to do for you?*

God is in the business of faithfulness. What do you want God to do for you that you cannot do for yourself? What do you want God to do that no one else can do for you? What do you want God to do for you that will declare to the world that He is real?

What do you want?

THOUGHTS FROM A THERAPIST

Dr. Deb on *Why*

——

Most people don't realize we actually make decisions from the emotional, nonlinguistic part of our brain: the limbic system. It's our neocortex, the most complex operating system of our brain, that rationalizes and puts words to our decisions, but the deciding part is initiated by our feelings.

If you're stuck not knowing what you want, consider the *why* first. Let's use Bianca's story as an example. Her *what* was ten thousand dollars, and her *how* was praying for God to miraculously produce those funds in seven days. However, it was her *why*—the vision to start a church to reach the lost and unloved—that inspired the passionate reaction within herself and in those who witnessed the pastor's generosity. It was the *why* that reminded her of God's faithfulness and drew her closer to Him in a time of anxiousness and uncertainty.

When we allow our *why* to inform our *what* instead of the other way around, we're less likely to miss the ways in which God answers our prayers because we conform our hearts to the desire of His.

CHAPTER 12

DEPRESSED, STRESSED, AND BITTER

"Call me Mara, because the Almighty has made my life very bitter."

RUTH 1:20

The walls were white and sterile. The hum of an old television filled the air with white noise. Expired magazines sat on a dented coffee table and half-stapled inspirational posters hung limply against the wall. It was a hospital, but someone had feebly attempted to make it feel like a home. The pot in the corner filled the room with the faint scent of old coffee, and mismatched mugs were strewn about the room.

A man came to the waiting room wearing white scrubs, the uniform for the employees of the psych ward. He extended his hand formally, said his name was Marco, and then quickly escorted me beyond the electronically dead-bolted doors. We walked down long, windowless corridors bereft of décor. I tried to listen to Marco as he shared details about Chloe, the girl I was visiting, but his words sounded muddled in my ears. Something about . . .

Depression.

Panic attacks.

Anxiety.

Anorexia.

Suicide.

Suicide. The word jerked me back to reality. Chloe had tried to kill herself, at just seventeen years old. I was only twenty-two myself and felt wildly underqualified to speak with her as a "spiritual adviser."

The secretary from my church had called and asked if I would do a hospital visit. Chloe's aunt attended my church, too, and was desperate for someone to visit with Chloe, who lived in Orange County. Since I served in youth ministry, I volunteered, but I had no idea where I was going or why. When I pulled into the gravel driveway, passing the guarded gate and the sign that read "Juvenile Psych Ward," I felt like maybe it was more than I'd bargained for.

Currently in the US, one in five adults experience mental illness, and ten million adults live with a serious mental illness that impacts their day-to-day functioning.[1] There are twice as many suicides as homicides in the US, and suicide is the second leading cause of death among individuals between the ages of fifteen and thirty-four. While it's difficult to determine how many people suffering from mental-health-related disorders go undiagnosed, the World Health Organization suggests that 55 percent of people do not have access to or receive treatment.[2]

Marco told me he would remain outside the room in case things got violent or dangerous. I smiled and thanked him while trying to silence the inner voice that was screaming, *What are you doing? Run away right now!*

I crept slowly into the room. My eyes met Chloe's, and I smiled. She was lying in her hospital bed and tried to sit up as I entered, but her arms were heavily bandaged because of her injuries, and precautionary restraints prevented her from moving much at all.

When she asked me to help her sit up, I located the bed's remote and adjusted it so she sat, ever-so-slowly, upright. Then, because I am keenly skilled at making awkward situations even more awkward, I hugged her and said, "Hi, Chloe! How are you?"

She smiled graciously as she gestured to her bandages. "I've been better."

We laughed. The ice was broken.

Marco popped his head in and asked if I wanted a chair, which I did, and as I made myself comfortable, Chloe and I began to get to know each other. We chatted about music, movies, and which pop star was dating whom. It almost felt—if only for a moment—like we were old friends just catching up.

Having never done a hospital visitation before, I had no clue what I was supposed to say. But in hindsight, my clear lack of agenda may have been exactly what Chloe needed. If I had shown up with a script or list of some spiritual platitudes to give her, I might as well have tried to heal a bullet wound with a Band-Aid. Instead, I sat down and unintentionally reminded her what it felt like to be alive, to be heard, to be loved. That maybe, just maybe, she could experience a life worth living.

I called for Marco like he was a poolside cabana boy and asked if he could grab us some snacks. Chloe loved that I told Marco what to do and laughed as he rolled his eyes at us. After five cups of red Jell-O and three episodes of *Judge Judy*, Chloe said, "I didn't have anyone to talk to." Placing my empty Jell-O cup and plastic spoon on her food tray, I asked her what she meant.

"I know you're wondering why," she said. "Why I'm here. Why I tried to take my life. Why I don't want to live. But how do you expect someone who is drowning to explain their feelings? Drowning people can't talk. They can't scream because they don't even have air to breathe. That's the way it feels. That's the way it feels when you would rather end the pain than struggle to live. I was drowning, Bianca. And no one helped me."

Chloe spoke about her father's affair, her parents' impending divorce, and the ensuing custody battle. She told me about the boys she slept with out of anger at her parents. She described how she first heard about cutting and the momentary reprieve it provided. She spilled the details about the pills she popped—pills I'd never even heard of. But the most unexpected part was the isolation she'd felt when she tried going to church. She walked into the sanctuary and no one greeted her or asked her name. She sat in the back and listened to a sermon from the pastor on joy while she was feeling nothing but total sadness.

After the service, she decided to listen to the pastor's invitation to *receive the joy of the Lord* and went to meet with someone on the volunteer prayer team. When she shared her overwhelming feelings of depression and anxiety, the prayer partner grabbed her hand, interrupting her, and said, "There, there, sweetheart. The joy of the Lord will be your strength. Let's pray."

As if a verse a day will keep the depression away.

I choose to believe that prayer team volunteer had the best of intentions. But without the ability to listen and love in the midst of pain, we will never be able to empathize with someone, to sit with them and simply listen out of love. Words like *depression* and *mental illness* sometimes carry the same stigma as the lepers and the outcasts of Jesus's day, even though they shouldn't. Sure, we may feel badly about someone's plight, but who really knows what to *do* with them? We may figuratively pat their heads or look on them with pity from what seems a safe distance, or say things like, *There, there, you will be all right*—but *will* they? If we don't sit with them, talk with them, love them, and believe for their healing in Jesus's name, will they be all right? And what if we feel *we* are the proverbial lepers and outcasts? Is there really a "There, there" solution that can make it all better?

Bitter Old Lady or Depressed Woman of Sorrow

Depression figures prominently in many stories from the Old Testament. Listen to the painful words of Naomi:

> So the two women went on until they came to Bethlehem. When they arrived in Bethlehem, the whole town was stirred because of them, and the women exclaimed, "Can this be Naomi?"
>
> "Don't call me Naomi," she told them. "Call me Mara, because the Almighty has made my life very bitter. I went away full, but the LORD has brought me back empty. Why call me Naomi? The LORD has afflicted me; the Almighty has brought misfortune upon me." (Ruth 1:19–21)

What is your first reaction to Naomi? Many Bible commentators make assessments about Naomi's bitterness and harp on the idea that we aren't supposed to be bitter. *Bitter is bad! Naomi is bitter! Therefore Naomi is bad!*

The authors of Hebrews and Ephesians warn us against bitterness, but there is something powerful about Naomi's honesty. If we are honest, we all go through seasons that in some way resemble Naomi's. No matter what your theology, how much you love God, or how much Scripture you can quote, at some point you're not going to be happy with God because He didn't do what you asked or come through in the way you thought He would.

What's great about Naomi is that she has the courage to *say* it. How many times have you sat in church angry, bitter, frustrated, and upset, but the moment someone asks you how you're doing, you smile and say, "I'm fine"? That is a lie and you know it! When your small group consists of Ben & Jerry, you might be eating your emotions. If your prayer circle is composed of Jim Beam, Johnnie Walker, and Jose Cuervo, you might be drinking your sorrows. Don't lie. Don't hide. Don't pretend you're fine when you aren't. We get the word *hypocrisy* from the Greek word for *actor*, or, literally translated, "one who wears a mask." As Christians we should know that masks do not belong on those who are part of the body of Christ.[3]

Naomi was candid about her station in life, even if it was uncomfortable for others to hear. And as she mourned, she shared her grief in community, in the company of God's people. She said, "My life is horrible, God has forgotten me, and it feels like God is upset with me." If she were to say that, drunk, at a bar at 2 a.m., we might simply guess this woman had lost her faith. But where was she? With God's people. This was the equivalent of Naomi showing up at small group, going to church, and being with friends, but at the same time honestly owning her grief and depression.[4]

Can we be women who do the same? And can we love those who—like Naomi—are in a season of lament?

Naomi provides an excellent example of this. Her depression stemmed from a series of traumatic losses (and, Dr. Deb would argue, she was suffering from post-traumatic stress disorder). She had to move away from her home due to the threat of famine, then her husband died, and shortly thereafter, her two sons. She was stuck in a foreign land, highly vulnerable as a single woman to a number of potential threats to her safety and well-being. She'd lost her social and spiritual support, her soul mate, and the provision of her sons in the aftermath of her husband's death.

As Dr. Deb asserts, the symptoms we see from Naomi in Ruth 1:13 include hopelessness, anger, and an increase in self-focused attention ("it is exceedingly bitter *to me* for your sake that the hand of the LORD has gone out against *me*" [ESV]). These are all indicators that Naomi was likely in a full-blown depressive state—understandably so! If we evaluate our own lives, we might find ourselves wrestling with the same kind of mental or emotional ailment.

With all this in mind, Dr. Deb and I have identified—based on the narrative and flow of Ruth's story of loss, rebuilding, and redemption—ways to navigate and address depression in three general categories below. Though these categories are not exhaustive, our intention is to provide language for talking about and suggestions for dealing with the onset of depression or anxiety.

1. Purpose

The excessive self-focus associated with depression can be a strong pull to keep people who are struggling in the depressive cycle stuck, repeating the same cycles. Discovering your purpose will make you want to do something bigger than yourself and sometimes bigger than your ability. But even the word *purpose* may feel nebulous and overwhelming. Some of us are lucky enough to be gripped by passions that keep us up at night, dreaming up pathways that will lead to quenching them. But others of us have far less certainty.

According to Dr. Deb, the biggest barrier to finding our purpose is overcomplicating and amplifying our expectations of what *purpose* is. "We equate purpose with impact, and we measure impact in digits that far exceed our ability and level of motivation, especially in times of depression. We're so focused on an invisible bigger picture that we're failing at our purpose before we can even identify it!" The inability to identify our purpose leaves us feeling hopeless, helpless, and discouraged. What if, instead, we simplified our purpose down to one modest, achievable action: *What is one tangible way I can show love in this moment?*

Naomi found purpose in looking outside herself and her situation by pouring herself into helping Ruth navigate her uncertain circumstances. Social psychologists have studied the impact of "pay it forward" – type helping and have found that outcomes for these helpers include empowerment, improved feelings of self-worth and well-being, and enhanced mental health.[5]

Not only did Naomi find purpose in pouring into Ruth (the next generation), but in baby Obed, her grandson (the next, next generation).[6] Finding a sense of purpose can come with pouring yourself into others. When we focus on others, we remove the self-focused attention that can perpetuate the cycle of depression.

So pare your purpose down to something achievable. You might ask the person in line behind you at the coffee shop how their day is going and listen to *understand*, not just to respond. Maybe you choose to play on the floor with your toddler despite the pull of a never-ending list of unfinished tasks. Consider reaching out to a friend and expressing gratitude for something they've done or for who they are in your life. Hold the door open for the mom struggling to push the stroller with the screaming kid out of the grocery store. Even if all you do is bite your tongue when you really want to throw your colleague under the bus for a sloppy job on the project report and instead offer a compliment, it can make a difference. Do something for someone else. Then do it again in the next moment.

Dr. Deb suggests that finding our purpose begins "by asking ourselves what we want to be known for and not limiting our response to the perfect job, relationship, or social status. We fulfill our purpose when we offer the same tangible act of love equally in the absence of an audience as in the presence of one."

When I met Chloe, she had no sense of purpose and confessed to me that she still didn't even want to live. She had intimately known the pain of isolation and the feeling of not wanting to survive if she couldn't thrive. But on her road to recovery, she discovered how much she loved bringing hope to children wrestling with depression. Through her pain, she discovered a sense of purpose. After college, Chloe went back to the hospital where she was institutionalized and began her clinical counseling practice, helping children just like her who needed hope and faith in seasons of darkness.

2. Community

This portion of the Ruth narrative begins and ends with the women of the community surrounding Ruth and Naomi. The community of women journeyed with Naomi *as she was*, instead of telling her *who* and *how* she should be. Unfortunately, as Christians, we're great at telling others who and how they should be, something we generally shouldn't do, even if we have the best of intentions.

It's hard to see our loved ones in pain and discomfort. We want to soothe, fix, and remove the problems that cause ongoing feelings of depression and hopelessness. Naomi's friends didn't say, "Now, Naomi, is Mara *really* how you want to go? God never gives us more than we can handle. Just trust God, and you'll get through this." No, Naomi's friends were willing to get uncomfortable with her and embrace her right where she was, bitterness and all.

If you are waiting for community to appear on your doorstep, be forewarned: it rarely happens like that. Sometimes, as in the case of Naomi, we must seek out what we need and be vulnerable about what we're going through. For trauma or clinical depression, I would highly suggest meeting with a licensed counselor or therapist. But for most of us in new seasons, we simply need to know someone cares and is willing to walk with us.

Please know I'm not trying to oversimplify this process. Finding friends is hard. Finding friends in hard seasons of life is even harder. But with wisdom and careful vulnerability (read: not spilling your guts out to the first person you meet), you might just find some to journey with you in life.

When I was thirty years old, I married Matt and instantly became a stepmom (or s'mom, as I prefer). I wrestled with isolation, not knowing where to find support as I tried to fill my new role. Nothing in my life was how I'd imagined it would be, and I found myself grieving my life choices and even questioning my marriage. Before I knew it, I was on an emotional ledge and debated walking away from everything. I knew I couldn't process this in isolation, so I reached out to a woman I knew who had been successfully s'moming for over ten years. Was making the phone call difficult and embarrassing? Did I feel vulnerable to admit I felt totally overwhelmed and clueless as to how to handle it all? ABSOLUTELY. But without community and an honest place to process, I would never have adapted to my new environment.

If community isn't knocking at your door, don't be afraid to go knock on someone else's door. Pick up the phone and reach out. Sometimes we must be the initiator and create our own communities. Be the friend you wish you had.

3. Acceptance

Naomi accepted what may not have been her ideal outcome and willingly embraced a new reality—one in which God *still* provided.[7] According to Dr. Deb, depression is persistent when we are unable to break the negative narrative cycles running through our minds.

My first three years of marriage were incredibly difficult. In addition to moving to a new city, living in a new home, becoming a new mom, and attending a new church, I started a new job working for a global antitrafficking organization, A21. Facing the reality of modern-day slavery daily was so incredibly overwhelming that I felt I was losing my identity. I found myself overeating and isolated. I had no clue I was dealing with depression, burnout, and anxiety. Encouraged by Matt, who told me I needed to meet with a counselor, I was able to find an amazing therapist who helped me accept, own, and even love the season I was in.

The wisdom my therapist uncovered in me has stuck with me years later. So much of our time is spent trying to get to what's great in the *next* that we miss what's good in the *now*. Don't miss out on what God is whispering to you today because of where you want to be tomorrow.

Let's look at the end of Naomi's story as our proof. If Naomi had surrendered to depression and refused to view her life from a new perspective—that God continued to show up in the midst of her grief and loss—she would have missed out on a beautiful ending to her story.

Don't miss out on what God is whispering to you today because of where you want to be tomorrow.

The women said to Naomi: "Praise be to the LORD, who this day has not left you without a guardian-redeemer. May he become famous throughout Israel! He will renew your life and sustain you in your old age. For your daughter-in-law, who loves you and who is better to you than seven sons, has given him birth."

Then Naomi took the child in her arms and cared for him. The women living there said, "Naomi has a son!" And they named him Obed. He was the father of Jesse, the father of David. (Ruth 4:14–17)

By His Stripes

As our conversation in the hospital room was coming to an end, Chloe cleared her throat and asked, "Do you think my decision to take my life was wrong? Do you think God still loves me?"

In that moment, I sensed that the question of wrong choices wasn't exactly what needed to be addressed in that moment. Shame and guilt will try to highlight our failure and weigh us down, taking us deeper into depression. I knew I needed to elevate the conversation and focus instead on what was *true*.

"Chloe," I said, "I didn't come here to preach a sermon to you.

But I need you to know one thing: Your cutting and scars will never remove the pain. But there is One who has been cut and whipped and bled for us. And I need you to know it is by HIS stripes we are healed."[8]

With tears rolling down her face, Chloe confessed that God had saved her the day she attempted suicide. Lying on the cold tile of her bathroom, floor covered in blood from her wrists and forearms, she called out to God. She wasn't sure He even existed, but she knew she was dying and needed Him to save her.

As she was losing blood and consciousness, in that most desperate state, she had uttered one word: *Jesus.* I still remember the way she said *Jesus.* It was as gentle as a feather falling from a bird; it floated off her lips. I began to cry and grabbed the fingers protruding from beneath the tangle of gauze bandages.

"I know Jesus saved my life," she said. "But I also know He *gave* me life. Bianca, I'm still angry and I don't want to live, but I believe I'm *supposed* to live. I'm not living for my parents or my friends; I'm choosing to live because God gave me a second chance—and I don't know why."

I rested my head on her bed and wept silently. I didn't know what to say. I had no words of comfort or clarity. All I could quietly utter was, "Jesus loves you so much. Jesus loves you so much. He loves you so much."

Ten years later, I still think of Chloe. I laugh at how naive and inexperienced I was, but how God was in the room and how, in that moment, He made us both whole and connected.

It's true I have never slit my wrists, but I have certainly found other damaging ways to escape my pain. I have not suffered suicidal depression, but I have felt depressed. I have not been institutionalized, but I have felt trapped. At some point, we've all felt, to some extent, *something* like Chloe. Therefore, it is imperative that we never judge, dismiss, or cast away those who are suffering alone. One day or another, we all need a community to walk with. We all need to be reminded of who we are and of God's plan for our lives.

Maybe you feel like Naomi or Chloe. Maybe you are feeling unseen by God or even hurting yourself. Know that you are not alone. Millions of people wrestle with depression and anxiety and need help to navigate it. In the following *Thoughts from a Therapist* section are some ways to identify depression and some actionable items to get help.

Maybe you feel like Ruth—with a heart to support a loved one who has withdrawn or isolated herself due to depression. Don't be afraid to initiate a conversation. Though this might feel incredibly intimidating, just use simple and honest language to express your concern, and then make yourself available to talk. Stay away from accusations or diagnoses, and instead listen, allowing your loved one space to open up and express what he or she is feeling.

As God met Naomi in Bethlehem, as God met Chloe on the bathroom floor, God wants to meet us right where we are. We can come to Him bitter or bloody, and He will right all our wrongs.

How do I know this? Because His bloodshed is stronger than any bitterness, depression, anxiety, or fear.

THOUGHTS FROM A THERAPIST

Dr. Deb on Depression

Depression can mask itself in a number of symptoms. To shed light on a difficult topic, here are ten signs you might be dealing with depression.

1. Feeling sad, lonely, empty, or a number of other emotions that leave you in a heavy or irritable mood (other people in your life may notice this)

2. Feeling or describing yourself as worthless
3. Feeling an excessive amount of guilt
4. A decreased desire to engage in things that you normally find energizing, fun, or pleasurable
5. Noticeable changes in weight (gain or loss)
6. Significant changes in your sleep habits (sleeping too much or difficulty falling or staying asleep)
7. Difficulty getting motivated to engage in everyday activities (getting to work, completing daily tasks, spending time in community)
8. Loss of energy or constant fatigue
9. Difficulty staying focused
10. Thoughts of harming yourself or suicidal thoughts

If you feel stuck in a prolonged period of depression (having such feelings more often than not over the course of two weeks), make an appointment to see your doctor. A primary care doctor can at least help with an initial screening to provide insight into whether or not you're experiencing clinical depression that might have biological roots and be best treated with medication and counseling. Before you go to your appointment, jot down some specific examples of where and how you're struggling, such as:

- "I'm not motivated to spend time with friends like I used to."
- "I have trouble getting out of bed most days."
- "My boss has made increasingly frequent comments about my diminished work performance."
- "I cry more days than not."

If your doctor doesn't have recommendations for an appropriate counselor, or you don't feel a doctor is necessary at this point, reach out to your church and ask if they have a list of local, vetted counselors they refer to. In a study done by LifeWay, 68 percent of pastors indicated that their church has a list of local mental health resources for church members, but only 28 percent of their congregation knew that list existed.[9] If your church doesn't have a list, check out a national database such as Psychology Today (https://www.psychologytoday.com). Their search engine allows you to choose a local area and specify a counselor with experience in working with a particular faith background. If you can't afford a professional, licensed counselor, see if a college or university in your area has a counseling center that employs graduate-level trainees. They often see clients at a reduced or pro bono rate. Even better, find a Christian college that's training counselors from a faith-based perspective.

You may have to try more than one counselor before you find the right fit. Be persistent in advocating for what works best for you. While it might be scary or overwhelming to think about sharing your story with a stranger more than once, the long-term outcome of finding someone you feel safe, comfortable, and able to be open with will far outweigh the momentary discomfort of sharing your struggles.

If this just feels too intimidating, make a commitment to open up to a friend, a family member, a pastor, or someone else you trust and can be vulnerable with. Loneliness and isolation are like oxygen on the fire of depression—they can worsen what you're already struggling with. Know that there is power and reprieve when a struggle is brought into the light. Speak your pain and let God reveal His purpose.

CHAPTER 13

YOU ARE THE ANSWER TO SOMEONE'S PRAYER

"May the LORD repay you for what you have done. May you be richly rewarded by the LORD, the God of Israel, under whose wings you have come to take refuge."

RUTH 2:12

"I'll pray for you," I said to Nicole on the way out of church. It's a phrase I say often. I usually pray right in the moment, so I can be sure to honor my word and remember a person's need. As I pulled Nicole close to me, I asked God that her stress would subside and that she would be able to find peace in the midst of her chaos. A single mom with two kids, Nicole had found solace in church after her divorce. What she still struggled to find was balance and a little bit of time to herself.

After catching up in the hallway outside the sanctuary, I knew Nicole just needed a break. She worked a full-time job and had two kids under five years old. Then, as I was praying for her to find rest and peace, something said to me, *Why don't you offer to watch her*

129

kids? She needs a break, so give her a break. But I pushed the thought aside and asked God to make a way for her.

No one intentionally tries to ignore people in pain (unless they are a psychopath or someone who kicks little dogs). But sometimes, in our busyness, we fall into dangerous patterns, repeating the same old go-to verses and walking through emotionless prayers by rote. We can get so used to the autopilot ritual of praying for each other that we stop believing *we* might actually be the answer to someone's prayer, the solution to someone's problem.

Throughout the entire book of Ruth, we see a specific theme that occurs in every chapter. It is the blessing of "loving-kindness" given as a prayer over those in need. The Hebrew word is *hesed*, a summation of the characteristics of God: loving, compassionate, kind, good.

So when Boaz blessed Ruth in chapter 2, verses 11–12, he essentially said, "Ruth, your character and reputation precede you. Everyone is talking about your hard life, but also how you love the Lord and have come here to live among God's people. I have heard you've been loyal and faithful to your mother-in-law, which is so honorable. I pray God will provide for you with food, friends, and family."

Boaz, a man of stature and status, publicly blessed a barren Moabite widow. His prayer of loving-kindness (*hesed*) was asking God to provide what Ruth had lost: a home, a family, a husband, a baby, and a future.

Sometimes prayer changes the heart of the one who is asking.

There are many functions of prayer, but the one I want to focus on is this: Sometimes prayer changes the heart of the one who is asking.

I want to reiterate something I mentioned briefly before. After Boaz prayed that Ruth would be rewarded by God for her faithfulness, he effectively answered his own prayer. Boaz prayed that God would protect and care for Ruth. Was that prayer answered? Yes. Who did God send to answer the prayer of Boaz? Boaz! I will argue, based on this text, that sometimes we will answer our own prayers.

While praying for Nicole, I dismissed the idea that I might offer her anything other than the prayer itself.

It wasn't until a few days later that I realized how absurd that was. Sure, I couldn't pay preschool fees for Nicole's children, but I *could* clean her house. I wasn't available as a permanent nanny, but I *could* babysit for a night. So that's exactly what I did. Like Mary Poppins, I came in with a big bag of tricks (aka cleaning supplies, DVDs, and junk food for the kids) and sent Nicole out for a manicure. In no way was I trying to be a savior or a fixer, but I knew surely there was *something* I could do to help her. As Boaz prayed for Ruth to experience God's *hesed*, I prayed for Nicole to experience the same blessing. As it turned out, that meant me answering my own prayer.

Sometimes we shy away from helping because we feel our help is inconsequential or meaningless. But *hesed* is never without effect. We might be the answer to someone's problem. We might be the solution to someone's issue. We might be the *hesed* we are praying for. Be brave and look for ways to help those in need. Maybe you have a friend who's struggling with her weight and lack of motivation. What would it look like to reach out and go for a walk together? Maybe you have a family member struggling financially. Could you send them a note and a gift card to make them feel loved? It might not feel like a big donation to you, but in a moment of lack it might feel like a divine provision to them.

Small gestures feel like big love. You've got this!

CHAPTER 14

SANCTIFIED AFFLICTION

"It is more bitter for me than for you, because the
*L*ORD*'s hand has turned against me!"*
RUTH 1:13

Not only have I felt confused by God but, like Naomi, I've had moments when I felt like God had turned His back against me. I went through one of the hardest seasons of my life when I was dumped by the man I thought I was going to marry while I was struggling to ace the last of my college finals and simultaneously coping with my mother's brain cancer diagnosis and estimated 30 percent chance of survival. In that season I questioned the goodness of God, the power of God, and the kindness of God. I felt like He had turned His back on me.

Maybe you resonate with that struggle. Perhaps you have found yourself saying, "God, I know I did *this* and they did *that*, but You should have showed up! You could've warned me. But You didn't, and now I'm here." The bitter words that came from Naomi's lips indicate that she saw God not as friend, but as foe.

As children of God, we know life isn't going to be easy. Even Jesus warns us of the trouble and trials we will face in our lives.[1]

While very few theologians have ventured to explore the subject of God's providence via the doctrine of affliction (read: why bad things happen to good people), in his book *The Mystery of Providence*, Puritan theologian John Flavel theorized that for followers of Christ, there is such a thing as "sanctified" affliction.[2] Through our pain and trials, we have the ability to be transformed.

Everything must pass through the hand of God. And God, who is in control of all (sovereign), can either act or not act. He can intervene or not intervene. He can allow blessing or allow hardship to come upon us. He is sovereign.

What that means for a believer in God is that whatever affliction we face—loss, pain, trial, or illness—will serve an entirely different purpose than it would for a nonbeliever who is suffering the exact same thing.

According to Puritan theologians like Flavel, an affliction can sanctify us—set us apart. It is through affliction that God uses whatever we are facing to make us more like the Lord Jesus. In surviving the fires of affliction, we are transformed. Our faith and intimacy with God are deepened as we choose to believe He is good and in control, even when our lives seem to be flying off the rails.

So when we find ourselves where Naomi found herself—dealing with loss, managing transition, grieving death—we must reconcile ourselves to the fact that we will not have all of our questions answered in this life. But in the life to come, as Paul writes to the Corinthian church, we will know in full.[3]

One of the best questions we can ask in these tough seasons is, "God, what are you trying to teach me through this?" Because this is what I do know:

There is no affliction . . .

There is no poverty . . .

There is no loss . . .

There is no pain . . .

There is no weeping . . .

There is no shedding of tears . . .

There is no brokenness . . .

. . . There is nothing in the life of a child of God that is pointless, purposeless, or past redemption.

If we have this view and are willing to actively seek the growth and change our trials are pushing us toward, we will change the way we suffer. We will equip ourselves for life's struggles. We will be empowered to shout at our fear and our pain and our confusion and say, "If it isn't redeemed, then God isn't finished." When I look back at some of the hardest times of my adult life—dealing with my mom's brain cancer, the sudden death of my beloved grandmother, or my husband losing his job—I believe those hardships have strengthened my faith. If our bodies get stronger when we put them under stress, why would our spiritual lives be any different? Every hardship will be won back by God for His glory and our good. I'm a living witness of and testament to it!

If you don't see your struggles this way yet, don't worry. Naomi didn't, either. So just as she was honest in her questioning, doubting, and bitterness, you are free to feel those same feelings! It's normal. As we read the end of Ruth and Naomi's story—and as we live out our own stories—we will see how God is both sovereign *and* good.

Struggles aren't always consequences for poor decisions. Sometimes they are—there's nothing like the regret we feel after a weekend full of bad choices. But struggles refine us and are our best chances to hear God's voice. As C. S. Lewis said, "God whispers to us in our pleasures, speaks in our conscience, but shouts in our pain."

CHAPTER 15

TIME TO SAY GOODBYE

Now Elimelek, Naomi's husband, died . . . both
Mahlon and Kilion also died, and Naomi was left
without her two sons and her husband.

RUTH 1:3, 5

She was the matriarch of our family. Dark-haired, fair-skinned, fashionable, and always on time, my grandmother left Puerto Rico to build a new life in New York. She found a job working in a factory, sewing for hours on end. As a seamstress, she constructed clothes she would never be able to afford. Each morning she walked into work with neatly coiffed hair only to have it flattened by her own perspiration in a hot Manhattan workshop—a *sweatshop*, really.

But she wasn't fazed. This was America, the land of dreams.

She met a man who made her a wife, had three children, and moved to Los Angeles where, the word was, jobs were better, winters were milder, and rents were lower.

Living in a new city brought the promise of change, but before she knew it, my grandmother had, once again, found a job working in a factory, sewing for hours on end. As a seamstress, she constructed clothes she would never be able to afford. Each morning she walked into work with neatly coiffed hair only to have it flattened by her own perspiration in a hot ~~Manhattan~~ Los Angeles workshop—a *sweatshop*, really.

And still, she wasn't fazed. This was America, the land of dreams.

Before the sun rose each day, she was up making strong coffee, packing lunches, and walking her children to school so she could catch a series of buses that would take her downtown for her ten-hour workday. Exhausted and achy, she commuted back home to cook *arroz con gandules*, *tostones*, and *bacalao* for her family. After they were all asleep, she would wash uniforms for her children and press the shirt her husband inevitably mussed with paint and turpentine while he painted houses in the blazing sun. Day after day, month after month, year after year, she gave selflessly for her family because she believed these were the sacrifices that were necessary to live in her land of dreams.

Decades later, my grandmother moved in with my parents for what she intended to be a short transition period after my grandfather died. It was there that she got sick. What started as a common cold gave way to the flu. Then it was bronchitis. And then she was gone. Out of nowhere, the woman who sewed her entire life came apart at the seams. I watched my grandmother gasp for breath as emergency room doctors tried to save her. She whispered, *Ya me voy*. And just as she said, *she left*.

Death is a devastating thing. If you're a Christian, you might know Paul's words of encouragement surrounding death: "Where, O death, is your victory? Where, O death, is your sting?" (1 Corinthians 15:55) But just as we can't simply put a Band-Aid over a bullet wound, we can't slap a Bible verse on deep suffering and just make it go away. Even when we trust there is new life in Jesus, that doesn't mean deep suffering won't occur.

Following my grandmother's sudden and unexpected death,

I was reeling with questions and confusion. *Why was her life taken so tragically and painfully? How could God allow this to happen to such a good person?*

I wasn't the first to ask these questions, and I certainly won't be the last. They, and many like them, have been asked for centuries from the mouths of the faithful and the faithless alike.

Death isn't something most of us like to talk about. If you're under thirty years old, it's something you probably rarely discuss. But whether we acknowledge it or not, death will happen, and sometimes it will occur more often and in more ways than we realize.

We might experience the death of a dream.

We might face the death of a marriage.

We might encounter the death of friendship.

We might go through the death of a business venture.

How can we survive the death—physical or emotional—of a relationship, a loved one, or even ourselves?

Let's take a look at Naomi and how she dealt with death.

Picture Naomi in the city of Moab shoveling dirt over the body of her son, Kilion, who was buried next to her other son, Mahlon, who was buried next to her husband, Elimelek. What was she thinking with every scoop of dirt that landed on the graves?

What will we do now?

Why did God allow this?

How do we move on from here?

Death and grief are overwhelming, and during Naomi's time, in her culture, the loss of a spouse and sons created an additional burden. A husband signified and guaranteed protection, financial security, and land. Men held authority in the community to make decisions, vote, and buy property. The loss of Naomi's husband would have dealt a devastating blow to her psyche and her security. The loss of her sons would not only have broken her heart, it would have robbed her future of hope.

Naomi lost everyone who came with her to Moab. A piece of her heart was buried six feet under, three times over.

When people, relationships, or dreams die, we *must* mourn. We live in a society that hands people tissues at the faintest sign of a tear. We pat backs and tell each other not to cry. We take a single day off work for bereavement and expect life to resume as usual. It doesn't. It *can't*. But we need to know how to process through grief in order to live healthy lives in the midst of pain and loss.

> With her two daughters-in-law she left the place where she had been living and set out on the road that would take them back to the land of Judah.
>
> Then Naomi said to her two daughters-in-law, "Go back, each of you, to your mother's home. May the Lord show you kindness, as you have shown kindness to your dead husbands and to me. May the Lord grant that each of you will find rest in the home of another husband."
>
> Then she kissed them goodbye and they wept aloud. (Ruth 1:7–9)

Naomi suffered in ways I hope none of us ever have the ability to fully relate to.

But I believe we can learn valuable lessons from this woman who lost everything and lived to talk about it.

Lessons on Grief

1. Acknowledge Reality

Naomi lost everything. Her home, her husband, and her hope were mere memories from Moab. She needed—as we all do—the space to acknowledge her new reality. Unafraid to admit her loss or honestly lament her life, Naomi said, "I went away full, but the Lord has brought me back empty. Why call me Naomi?

The LORD has afflicted me; the Almighty has brought misfortune upon me" (Ruth 1:21). Acknowledge your reality and your pain.

When we don't acknowledge reality, we sacrifice the sacred act of mourning that precedes divine healing. The Bible tells us that when Naomi kissed Ruth and Orpah goodbye, they *all* wept. There is something cathartic about the shared act of weeping.

2. Accept Reactions

If you find yourself in a position to comfort a friend who's grieving, remember, we all handle pain and loss differently. Just because I want to be hugged and held tightly during a time of loss doesn't mean my husband does. Part of walking with a loved one after loss is letting them grieve and mourn in their individual way.

Naomi was burdened by the loss of her livelihood and didn't want to pass that burden along to her daughters-in-law. She pushed them away emotionally and told them to go home—essentially saying, "Leave me and try to be happy and whole again. What can I offer you but sadness?"

It's important to recognize what's at play when a grieving person pushes you away. It likely isn't personal at all—that person might just need space. But don't let their need for space allow them to live in isolation. Be present. Send a note or a text with an encouraging word. Offer to drop off a meal. And always accept their reactions with grace and space. We all handle loss differently.

3. Avoid Remedying

In the midst of trial and trauma, there is often anger, despair, and depression. This is all part of the grief process (read: you're normal). If someone is yelling, weeping, or completely breaking down, don't try to stop them. Let everyone, yourself included, feel all the feelings. Numbing the pain with drugs, drink, or distraction can't solve anything long-term. Silencing tears that need to be cried will only prolong the grieving process.

When Naomi found herself overcome by despair on the desert road in Moab, neither Orpah nor Ruth asked her to be anything she wasn't. Ruth, by contrast, showed her love and support by accompanying Naomi on the journey back home.

As a reminder, the death of an elderly man doesn't hurt less than the death of a newborn baby. The breakup of a relationship doesn't hurt less if a person was cheated on. The loss of a job doesn't hurt less because the work environment was unhealthy. It is more important to acknowledge the pain and reality of loss than to attempt to find the silver lining you think might lessen the blow.

4. Affirm Reengaging

This is the toughest step, so give yourself grace. Life after loss can be disorienting, not just emotionally but physically as well. Lying in bed with the blinds drawn, eating chocolate, and scrolling through an ex-boyfriend's social media can be tempting means of comfort, but they aren't going to help the healing process. On the other hand, simple things like going on a walk, journaling your feelings, or engaging in regular activities like folding laundry or cleaning can help acclimate you to life after loss.

If you are supporting a friend who has suffered a loss, affirm the steps toward healing. Remember that moving on after a death can sometimes feel like learning to walk again. It will take time. It will be exhausting. It will cause frustration. But if you encourage and affirm reengagement for those whose lives will never be the same, you will, in essence, take the journey with them. And that makes all the difference.

If we know how to grieve well, we will heal well and more quickly. In addition to being able to survive pain and loss, I believe we can also know how to deal with those who will walk through the valley of the shadow of death. And you can let them know they need "fear no evil" (Psalm 23:4).

———

When my grandmother breathed her final breath, we all had to say goodbye to our dreams of a future with her. The hope I held on to then is a hope I pass along to those who also deal with pain and loss: "He will wipe every tear from their eyes. There will be no more death or mourning or crying or pain, for the old order of things has passed away" (Revelation 21:4).

Death will come; that is inevitable. But apart from the death that will end our physical lives, we need to be sure we know how to deal with the pain that causes something inside of us to die while we are still alive. There is One who will comfort us and who promised us life to the full (John 10:10).

PART 3

Adulting and Growing Up

According to Jane Solomon, a lexicographer at Dictionary
.com, the word *adulting* is usually used in reference to
"delayed development." This isn't just about physical age or
chronological age, but about mind-set and maturity level.
The definition of adulting is "to behave in an adult manner;
engage in activities associated with adulthood."

Whether adulting takes the form of meal planning,
doing your taxes, or paying your rent on time, the word
itself encompasses life as we know it once we've fully tran-
sitioned from being reckless children to grown women. But
let's be clear on one truth about adulting. It is *actually* req-
uisite. You're grown, you *have* to, and you don't get a pat on
the back for simply fulfilling basic responsibilities.

Adulting isn't always fun, and often, it isn't easy, but
to do it successfully we need to face our responsibilities
with a sense of real maturity. As life presents us with

disappointments and even tragedy, we can use these experiences to become stronger and more resilient.

In this final section, we'll learn what responsible womanhood looks like in terms of:

- Growing up
- Sharing what we have with others
- Finding a mentor
- Being responsible at work
- Emerging successfully into adulthood
- Creating the life you want to live tomorrow

Ruth faced obstacles that would have sent the faint of heart running for the Ben & Jerry's and blocking out the world with a *Real Housewives* marathon (oh, it's not just me?), but she battled through the pain and hardship, put in real effort, and reaped the benefits of her own clear-headed maturity. Join me as we learn, by her example, to develop some new tools that prepare us for our very own harvests!

CHAPTER 16

GOODBYE CHILDHOOD, HELLO WOMANHOOD

And Ruth the Moabite said to Naomi, "Let me go to
the fields and pick up the leftover grain."
RUTH 2:2

My living room was full of gorgeous and talented women, brimming with vision and optimism about what lay ahead. I, passionate about the next generation, had opened my heart and home to a small, select group of fierce females, who were chosen to be part of the In the Name of Love summer internship. They came from all over the country to participate in a three-month, intensive ministry training, and this was day one.

As I looked around the room, I remembered what it felt like to be their age, to wonder the same things, and dream the same dreams—dreams about life and love, purpose and passion. I thought to myself, *When I was their age, what did I need to hear?* I listened to their stories and arrived at the simple truth I wished someone had told me when I was their age. It would have saved me from embarrassment, prideful falls, humiliation, and the many naive mistakes I made while stepping into leadership roles inside and outside of the church:

There is a difference between women and little girls.

Physically, these differences are obvious—that doesn't require much discussion. But I'm talking about the maturing of soul, mind, and spirit. The apostle Paul put it this way: "When I was a child, I used to speak like a child, think like a child, reason like a child; when I became a man, I did away with childish things."[1]

In Hebrew culture, children become adults at the age of thirteen. However, just because someone legally becomes an adult doesn't mean they act like an adult. For Latinas, rites of passage happen before a crowd at a quinceañera, when a girl turns fifteen years old. American culture grants grown-up responsibilities to kids on their eighteenth birthdays. But just because we are culturally labeled adults doesn't mean we act like them.

This can be most evident in our spiritual lives. We may look, and sometimes even act, like mature, devout women of God, but in fact, we're little girls in our big sister's lipstick, masquerading as the women we have yet to become.

I gathered the interns around my dining-room table and had "The Talk." No, not *that* talk—this wasn't that type of party. But just as any adolescent girl needs a no-nonsense knowledge-drop to get a grip on handling hygiene, hormones, and harnessing her little lady lumps in a properly sized bra, young believers require a bit of *motherly* advice to guide their spiritual development. (And when I say "motherly," I mean "the cool young aunt whose birth was a surprise to your grandparents in their sunset years.")

What I love about Ruth is how clearly she moved toward spiritual maturity in the desert. During the journey to Bethlehem, she boldly claimed her God, her people, and her commitment. She had suffered some inconceivably major blows and still managed to make the difficult and very adult choice to rely solely on God.

When it must have seemed tempting to run, to regress, or to give up entirely, Ruth, like Paul, did away with childish things.

I felt called to help the interns around my table toward womanhood and usher them into spiritual maturity. As Naomi guided Ruth, I wanted to help these young women in the same way.

Are You a Little Girl or a Grown Woman?

We don't all begin our faith walks at the same point in our lives. We don't all face the same challenges, and we certainly can't all expect to have access to the same support systems and opportunities. But as with any growth process, we need guidance from those who have gone before us in order to transition fully into who we're meant to be. Over the years (with the ever-helpful aid of my 20/20 hindsight) I've distilled some of my most useful lessons on adulting into the paragraphs below. Some of these I had to learn the hard way, and my hope is that you won't have to. And since I was raised on *Sesame Street* (a quintessential part of *my* growth), they will all start with the same letter, because this chapter is brought to you by the letter *P*. You're welcome.

1. Process

When we are young and immature, we tend to focus on praise and promotion, but a grown woman sees the importance of her *process*. What we learn through our work, and even by the act of simply doing that work, is far more important than any reward, increased status, or affirming words we may receive as a result.

After I finished teaching at the Rock Church in San Diego once, senior pastor Miles McPherson asked me if I'd ever had a speech coach review my sermons. I thought he was asking because he was so impressed by my awesome wordsmithing and polished prose. When I proudly told him I hadn't, he asked me if I wanted some feedback. *Um . . . excuse me?* I was hurt and embarrassed at my need for correction, especially following what felt like a really solid spin behind the pulpit. But where would that embarrassment get me? What good would a "Great job, Bi" have done when I had so much room to improve? I swallowed my pride and seized the opportunity to learn from one of the best.

Miles's feedback was brutally honest but incredibly helpful. And while it did make me a bit uncomfortable, I was well aware of how little a person grows when she stays inside her comfort zone. As a grown woman and communicator of the gospel, I knew I needed to receive Miles's insight as an investment in my maturing process. It made me better at my job, and, subsequently, better at my *life*.

Where was Ruth when Boaz saw her? Was she on Instagram trying to become a #Model? No, she was gleaning in the field and sweating like a pig on a roast. She wasn't looking for a pat on the back. Ruth was doing what she needed to do to survive and succeed. Because of her commitment to working and not whining, she was in a position to be promoted from worker to wife.

Put your head down and do the work.

Put your head down and do the work.

Don't worry about the promotion; focus on the process. Don't quit the painful process because you are addicted to praise. The process will mature you to focus on the future and build it rather than looking back longingly at an idyllic past.

2. Produce

Immaturity produces entitlement and negativity; grown women produce. Immaturity will cause us to focus on what we lack, but it takes an adult perspective for us to begin to work with what we have. If we are busy doing that work, we won't have time to focus on what we don't have.

Never do we hear Ruth complain. She was homeless, barren,

widowed, and suddenly responsible to provide for her aging mother-in-law in a land that wasn't her own. I don't think anyone would have blamed her if she'd collapsed into a heap and moaned all day. But instead of letting these struggles get the best of her, Ruth marched down to a field, got herself a job, and began to produce. If you've been given olives, make olive oil. If it's sour grapes, make wine. When you get lemons, make lemonade. **Use what you have to get what you want.**

It's not about what you have or don't have. It's about what God can do with whatever you give Him.

3. Payment

Every great leader, boss, preacher, teacher, or mom needs a coach. This person will pour into your life and help you become better. When we invite someone into our lives who can provide loving and thoughtful correction, we become better. A word of caution: be intentional about who you invite in. If you allow someone who is jealous of or threatened by you to speak into your life, it may cause a weakening in your confidence. Surround yourself with people who are *for* you, *love* you, and will be *honest* with you.

Grown women should view correction as a payment into their development. Little girls will make you pay for correcting them. And dealing with a payback from an immature child is the worst!

4. Purpose

A mature woman will declare she has purpose and potential living on the inside of her. She won't make excuses for who she is (and isn't).

We can either grow into all that God has called us to be, or we can make excuses for why we're not growing.

Ruth had every reason to sit at home, wallow, and complain, "I used to have a husband, but now I'm all alone and nobody wants me. I'm just a Moabite woman who is living among Jews who hate

Moabites. I'm only a barren widow who has nothing." *Just* and *only* are words that will keep us repeating the cycle and making excuses that we will never have enough.

> We must be women who declare and believe that we were created *on* purpose and *for* a purpose.

God's call is always found in our God-given talents and God-inspired passions and burdens for the world. And it requires spiritual maturity to ask ourselves: *When I breathe my last breath, will I have optimized those talents? Will I have done my best, throughout my lifetime, to get the highest return on His investment in me?*

Purpose exists when our gifts, experiences, and passions come together.

We must be women who declare and believe that we were created *on* purpose and *for* a purpose.

Just Like Jesus

The In the Name of Love internship program was a great learning exercise for all of us. And even as I oversaw the ministry, I discovered plenty of areas in my own leadership (and life) that were in need of some growth. But being "grown" in this sense is not an *end* in itself. Acting like a grown woman means believing and behaving in line with the reality that there will *always* be more room to grow. And for what it's worth, this includes generously giving grace to each other because we are all works in progress.

Luke wrote that "Jesus kept increasing in wisdom and stature, and in favor with God and men" (Luke 2:52 NASB). If our Lord and Savior had time to mature and grow in grace from others, and to give others grace to grow, we should do the same.

CHAPTER 17

MENTORING: DON'T WALK AWAY

But Ruth replied, "Don't urge me to leave you or to turn back from you. Where you go I will go, and where you stay I will stay."

RUTH 1:16

Three months into my job at A21, I found myself in more and more executive meetings. My boss began trusting me with bigger projects and shorter deadlines, and put me at the helm of a full company rebrand. But I had never led at the management level before. I felt like I was in over my head and wildly uncertain how to grow a team. It was painfully clear that I needed help.

The word *mentor* was more than a little intimidating to me. I always feared that having a mentor meant having to check in on a weekly basis with someone threatening me like a parole officer. When it was discussed in church, it always sounded more daunting than helpful, requiring endless classroom hours and a giant, ten-pound textbook. I *did* want a mentor, but I didn't want a class; I wanted a relationship with someone I admired, wanted to emulate, and from whom I could learn.

My insecurity told me just to read an article or two online, binge-watch *Oprah's Master Class*, or listen to a leadership podcast and call it a day. I wanted to be able to grow, but I didn't want to be vulnerable and admit I was struggling. But when I saw Robin at church one Sunday, all that changed.

Robin was one of the executive pastors at the church we attended, and I loved how she lived her life. The mother of two grown kids, wife to a strong, confident husband, and a business owner, she seemed to move effortlessly through life while maintaining a powerful walk with God. As we chatted, Robin mentioned a group of executive women to which she belonged. They met regularly to be counseled on strategies to navigate leadership, ministry, and business.

I was shocked.

Robin needed a coach to help navigate life? If ROBIN RILEY needed a coach, then good grief, I needed a team of them.

I asked Robin if I could have information about her group, and she explained that membership came by invitation only. "However," she offered graciously, "if you ever want to talk about leadership or life, my office is always open."

I casually thanked her and said goodbye, but internally I was giddy with excitement. I WAS GOING TO HAVE A MEETING WITH ROBIN RILEY! I felt so honored to have the offer of Robin's time so I could learn from her years of experience. And while I would have loved it if we became besties and braided each other's hair at weekend slumber parties, I had to recognize that Robin was not my peer. She, as any mentor, was a seasoned and successful coach who deserved to be treated with distinction.

The Mentor

Ruth witnessed her mother-in-law survive tragedy. As Ruth's own life led her through similar trials, she must have seen the value of learning from a woman who'd gone before her. When Ruth pledged to Naomi,

"Where you go I will go, and where you stay I will stay," she essentially made a commitment to learn from Naomi's life experiences.

Though our lives and situations may be vastly different from those of Ruth and Naomi, there is something to learn about mentoring from their relationship. Ruth could have returned to Moab when Naomi gave her the chance, returning to the place she'd always known to remain the woman she'd always been. She would have been absolved of any responsibility to her mother-in-law and free to marry someone else. Think about the humility involved in her decision to do otherwise. Ruth made herself vulnerable to a world of unknowns and committed to whatever challenges a life in Bethlehem would bring. A good mentee is willing to be humble, to accept correction, but a *great* mentee is dedicated to putting into practice the wisdom shared by a mentor.

How to Find a Mentor

You might not feel the need for a mentor, but there will be seasons in life when you'll know you need wisdom and insight from someone who has gone before you. Here are some tips from Dr. Deb and me to help you navigate how to find the perfect mentor for *you*.

1. Intentionality

Mentorship at its core requires intentionality. Being clear and decisive in your wants and needs is a critical first step in finding a mentor. Ask yourself these questions:

- What are the decisions or challenges in which I find myself consistently stuck?
- Where in my life do I need an objective voice and different perspective?

These answers will provide insight into the type of mentoring relationship you need. Do you need a career mentor? A spiritual mentor? Mentoring can help us grow in countless areas, from health and fitness to interpersonal relationships.

Once you've established the type of mentor you are looking for, be intentional in casting your net wide in the search process. Consider your current relationship circles, including your family, friends, colleagues, and church members. It's amazing to discover who-knows-who-knows-who when you're willing to share your search and seek input from others. Perhaps your mom knows someone in her Bible study; maybe your friend's work boss meets just the right qualifications; or it could be your small group leader was mentored by an amazing woman. It takes just one right conversation to set the wheels in motion.

If your circle is small or not in the vein of development you hoped for, search out a professional who would be willing to coach you. This might require payment or a contract, but if you have the means, make the investment.

2. Get Uncomfortable

The reality is, the mentorship process is likely to feel uncomfortable at first. Asking a possible mentor out for coffee might cause you to feel flooded with fear of rejection, disappointment, or judgment. Make a commitment to act *regardless* of the emotions you feel. If you're willing to commit to acting *in opposition* to your emotions (the opposite of fear is confidence), you can overcome the barrier these emotions create. Acknowledge and validate your fear, but don't succumb to it by turning back. Instead, demonstrate confidence.

For those of you who need some context or language to jump-start a mentoring conversation, I'm including a script that might help you:

"I'm looking for a mentor who's walked through _____

and would be willing to share her wisdom and experience with me. I am encountering some challenges and would love to see personal growth in these areas. Could I treat you to a cup of coffee and talk about the possibility of us establishing a mentoring relationship?"

If the answer you receive is no, acknowledge the disappointment, understand that it may not be personal, and recommit yourself to the search process. If the answer is yes, be grateful and proactive. Don't put the responsibility on your potential mentor to pick a day, time, and location to meet.

Cinderella

I think you can approach the search for a mentor a lot like you'd approach shoe shopping. If you see a pair you like but, say, the color isn't your norm or the strap seems like it may pinch, that doesn't mean you shouldn't at least try them on. Go to coffee with someone who might *not* be your ideal mentor! You could be pleasantly surprised.

On the flip side, just because you love the way a shoe looks, that doesn't mean it's going to be a good fit. Stay focused on the practicality of what you need and let that be the primary parameter. Where do we really think we're going in those six-inch red heels, ladies? We're not Beyoncé.

Your potential mentor should be living in a way that's similar to how you want to live. In my case, I needed someone to help me manage upward (specifically, to communicate effectively with the CEO and executive director of my company) as well as cast vision downward (to ensure that my team and I were always on the same page). I needed to balance my ambition with realistic goals, advance the cause of our organization, and forge a healthy work-life balance. Robin was the perfect fit for me!

For what it's worth, I'm not opposed to mentors of the opposite sex. There's plenty to be learned from the men and women we admire. But there are limits to how well mentors of the opposite sex can help us address certain needs. For example, if your goal is to work on yourself as a wife or a career woman in a male-dominated field, there's no amount of male insight that can take the place of female experience.

Maybe you are a young mom struggling to find joy in a difficult season. Find a woman who has successfully raised her children and learn from her. If you want to grow spiritually and go deeper in your faith, find someone who is boldly living out their walk with Jesus. If you've struggled with eating disorders and are seeking a way out, find someone who intimately knows how to find fullness and satisfaction in healthy living.

As you begin to think about WHO you want to pour into your life, let me encourage you HOW to show up.

Arrive on Time

Nothing will telegraph a lack of respect more than keeping someone waiting. If someone has carved time out of her schedule to meet with you, make sure you are punctual. And if you're late, you had better have a good reason! I once met with a mentee who casually strolled in twenty minutes late with a venti iced coffee and said, "OhMuhGah! The line at Starbucks was SOOOO long." It might have been easier to forgive if she'd at least brought one for me, too, but the bottom line was this: she should have skipped Starbucks altogether. If you have a tendency to mismanage *your* time, don't make that someone else's problem.

Respect the Timeline

If your mentor has designated a one-hour time slot, don't try to push it longer. Be mindful of the clock, and unless she initiates a lengthier meeting, be prepared to end in a timely fashion. When your time is winding down, be sure to conclude the meeting on a positive note and thank your mentor for her time. Gratitude and an easy conversation will make her more prone to meet with you again.

Be Prepared

If you initiated the meeting, come prepared with what you would like to discuss. In fact, ask your mentor if you might send over some discussion topics in advance so that they feel prepared. I once met with a young woman who asked to speak about a possible work internship. That conversation turned into two and a half hours of her recounting some painful childhood traumas. I felt honored that she trusted me with her story, but ultimately, my day was hijacked, and I hadn't been emotionally or spiritually prepared for what occurred. It's important, especially for a first meeting, that both parties have similar expectations in order to ensure a mutual benefit.

Finally, do the work! If you will be going through a book together, make sure you read the content. If your mentor gave you homework, make sure it's completed. Don't waste a mentor's time by showing up unprepared.

Bring a Gift or Token of Thanks

I met with Robin once every two months, and I brought her lunch every single time. I knew she liked to eat clean and healthy, so I made sure to always bring her something delicious and nutritious. On her birthday, I sent her a bouquet of her favorite flowers as a small showing of gratitude for her time. If you aren't paying for mentoring or coaching services, a little token of thanks goes a long way!

The gift doesn't have to be big or expensive, but it will let your mentor know you appreciate their time. A card, coffee, or simply covering the check at lunch will indicate your appreciation.

After three years, Robin and I stopped our regular meetings due to changes in our schedules. But even now, I consider her my mentor from afar. As I became passionate about being a mentor myself, I invited Robin to meet my interns and share her wisdom with them. Standing back and watching that presentation provided me with yet another valuable lesson. It was truly a gift from God.

She mentored me.

I mentored them.

They will mentor others.

Mentoring is challenging and requires self-sacrifice, but when you share with others what you have discovered about life or leadership, you are able to pour into them what has been poured into you. If you've never mentored anyone, but there's someone you would like to bless by coming alongside her to share your experiences, don't be afraid to initiate or make yourself available for a coffee date. You know more than you think you do, and you will be blessed more than you can imagine when you help someone else navigate a new season.

WHAT IF THE SHOE DOESN'T FIT?

What happens if the mentor you thought would be perfect isn't the right fit? Avoid any bad breakups or premature walk-aways by setting an end date. For example, let your mentor know how many meet-ups would be ideal:

- "Since you are free once a month, how about we connect for the next three months if that works for you?"
- "I love that you are giving me one day a week for phone calls! How about we meet once a week for six weeks?"

This way, you aren't committing to a long-term relationship. If it turns out you are a perfect pair, you can always ask for more time, but starting with an established end date releases both you and your mentor from a tricky conversation if either of you doesn't feel like it's working.

Mentoring is hard, so don't be hard to work with. You might feel frustrated by the way your mentor challenges you and even be tempted to walk away. Don't! You're in this relationship to grow, and growth won't come without growing pains. Accept the wisdom you're being offered, honor the leadership you're being given, and stay committed to the process.

CHAPTER 18

BE A STRONG WOMAN

*So Naomi returned from Moab accompanied by
Ruth the Moabite.*

RUTH 1:22

Kayla was bright and bold, a recent college grad with determination who asked a serious question at a roundtable forum where I spoke: "How do I interpret being identified as a 'strong' woman?" She described how, in a year-end work evaluation, she had been called a strong woman, and wrestled with the implication of that being a negative thing.

As the book of Ruth opens, our heroine is clearly identified as "Ruth the Moabite." Original readers of this account would have understood the derogatory implications of that phrase. To make sure we grasp the implications in modern language, consider that she might have been called "Ruth, the girl from the gutter." *Moabite*, though it identified Ruth's heritage accurately, was generally considered a negative term.

Now consider these words: *strong* and *woman*.

They're innocuous, even positive when spoken independently, but when strung together, they often take a pejorative tone. Even in today's culture, "strong woman" is, however absurdly, sometimes a euphemism for *pushy*, *bossy*, or *savage*.

What does a strong woman really look like? Using Ruth's life, let's explore how we can redefine and reclaim the term.

A STRONG WOMAN KNOWS WHO SHE IS. Emotional (weeping on the road back to Bethlehem) but committed (journeying with Naomi to Bethlehem), Ruth wasn't afraid to reveal her feelings (Ruth 1:14–18). Strong women are emotionally self-aware and understand their ability to withstand opposition.

A STRONG WOMAN FIGHTS AGAINST EXPECTATIONS. Aware of the obstacles in her way and the encouragement of her mother-in-law to go back to her hometown (Ruth 1:15), Ruth was not guided by fear. She chose to rebel against cultural expectations and pave a new path. Strong women are not dissuaded by norms and have the strength to go against what others expect.

A STRONG WOMAN PERSEVERES. Having lost home and husband, Ruth had every excuse to give up. However, in the face of famine and survival, the Moabitess went to work (Ruth 2:2). Strong women get back up every time they fall and push forward even in the face of great odds.

A STRONG WOMAN IS HUMBLE. Aware of the favor accorded to her by Boaz, Ruth was filled with gratitude and humbly bowed before him to thank him for his generosity (Ruth 2:10). Ruth's position of humility wasn't a sign of weakness, but rather an awareness of her dependency on others. Strong women aren't embarrassed to acknowledge how others have helped them and humbly give credit to those who have assisted.

A STRONG WOMAN ISN'T AFRAID TO ASK FOR WHAT SHE WANTS. Ruth knew her livelihood and another shot at love and a family were dependent upon Boaz. With some wisdom and coaching from Naomi, Ruth brazenly asked Boaz to take her and be her guardian redeemer, aka husband (Ruth 3:9). Assertive and bold, Ruth—a foreigner, widow, and field worker—went against the cultural norm to ask for what she wanted. Strong women are bold and brazen about asking for what they want. (Go back and read chapter 7 for a reminder!)

Appropriate the Language

What I explained to my new friend Kayla at the roundtable forum was that offense is a choice. The intention of her label at work was meant to be derogative. But when we appropriate and redefine stereotypes, a label like *strong woman* is an honor, not an insult.

Language is used not only to communicate realities, but also to convey insinuations. For example, when Christ ascended to heaven and His followers walked the earth proclaiming His glory, the public and those in power referred to Jesus's followers as "Christians," literally meaning *little Christs*—those who emulated and followed Him. It was intended to be derogatory. It was intended to be embarrassing. It was intended to be hurtful.

But to paraphrase Joseph in Genesis 50:20, what people intend for evil, God will use for good. Early Romans wanted to stigmatize and ostracize Christians. In the same way, those who are threatened by *strong women* often use this phrase in an attempt to insult us. But to take offense is a choice. And while the term *Christian* was intended to demean the early Church, early Christians wore the insult as a title with pride, embracing what it meant to them to be called followers of their Savior. Millennia later, I, too, wear that title not as an insult, but as a compliment.

When we appropriate language, we claim it for our own use. And we don't need the permission of anyone who intended it to be derogatory. We can take a word or phrase that was meant to dishonor us and assign to it our own meanings, then inhabit those meanings proudly.

We have no reason to take offense when we are called strong women. We *should* be strong women. We're called to be unwavering in our convictions, committed to truth, fiercely determined, and unwilling to be silenced when God is urging us to speak. We should be strength personified.

When everyone in the office is gossiping unfairly about a coworker, be a strong woman and shut it down. If your partner wants to make an unethical business move, be a strong woman and walk away. If there is a desire or dream within reach, be a strong woman and go after it.

Melinda Gates once said, "A woman with a voice is by definition a strong woman. But the search to find that voice can be remarkably difficult."[1] To those who feel silenced, squashed, or scared, I say be like Ruth. Act boldly in the face of fear, know who you are, be hungry and humble. But most importantly, don't be afraid to go after what you want.

CHAPTER 19

SHARING IS CARING

*Ruth also brought out and gave her what she had
left over after she had eaten enough.*

RUTH 2:18

When I was growing up in a family of seven, my mother constantly reminded us that sharing was not only biblical, it was a sign that we were growing up. How? She explained that true maturity is the realization that nothing we have is truly ours. When we understand that the blessings we have from God are not for us to possess but to *steward*, it changes how we live. In a culture that is very inwardly focused on self-help and self-preservation, sharing is a counter-cultural expression of maturity.

Linguists and child development experts will confirm that one of the first five words most children learn is *mine*. From a young age, we intrinsically struggle with sharing and the idea of giving away what we believe is ours. If left unaddressed, this pattern of selfishness can follow us into adulthood. As a result, we become spoiled grown children, trying to acquire and amass as much as possible, giving the least amount away.

According to the National Bureau of Economics, Americans

give away only 3.7 percent of our income.[1] But we aren't the only selfish ones. The Global Peace Index charts that some of the wealthiest nations are the least prone to give or share in proportion to their wealth. Someone with nearly nothing giving something to someone who has even less is a picture of complete selflessness.

This is exactly what we see in Ruth as she gives her unfinished meal to her mother-in-law after her lunch date with Boaz (Ruth 2:18). Ruth and Naomi were starving, and the first thought Ruth had was to share her meal with her mother-in-law. Her generosity and kindness are a learning lesson for us all!

Ruth had nothing but acquired something. She gave that something to someone with nothing. She was a sharer! Whether she always loved sharing, or learned to do it later on in her walk with God, Ruth demonstrated the importance of giving to those in need.

> And do not forget to do good and to share with others, for with such sacrifices God is pleased. (Hebrews 13:16)

Not only is God pleased, but our souls are, too! A 2008 study by Harvard Business School professor Michael Norton and colleagues showed that giving a sum of money away to someone else lifted people's well-being even more than spending it on themselves.[2] That sounds vaguely familiar, right? Jesus knew this all along, and it was radically countercultural even in His day when He told the church, "It is more blessed to give than to receive."[3] If the words of Jesus are right (when has He ever been wrong?!), giving people are happy people!

But what happens if you have never been properly taught how to share? What if giving wasn't something you were trained to do? You're in luck! Dr. Deb will show us the psychology of sharing and how we can employ it in our own lives.

THOUGHTS FROM A THERAPIST

Dr. Deb on Sharing

As kids, we focus on *mine*, and we hoard our things because we haven't yet developed confidence. *Confidence* communicates that we can trust in something or someone without question. Kids hold on to their favorite toy or their ragged, fluffy, one-eyed teddy bear because it provides them with security. And when they no longer have their security object, it feels as if they will never have security again.

Unfortunately, too often we carry this attitude into adulthood: *If I give _____ away, I might never get it back.* We develop an unconscious attitude that we must be utterly self-reliant. We hold so tightly to the idea of independence that the practice of dependence becomes shameful.

How do we challenge this mind-set and develop an embraced practice of sharing?

1. **COMMIT TO SHIFTING YOUR FOCUS FROM THE ACT OF GIVING TO THE EXPERIENCE OF RECEIVING.** Think about a time when you received something. Whether it was a gift, a free meal, or a word of advice, try to remember what that experience was like for you. When we give, too often we place the focus on ourselves. *What do we lose when we give?* But when we intentionally shift our focus to the experience of the receiver—the person who gets to eat our donated food, a coworker who enjoys the coffee we brought, the stranger who brightened up when we smiled—we can consider the impact our giving has on others instead of the impact it has on us.

2. **CHALLENGE THE WHY BEHIND YOUR MOTIVATION TO HOLD ON TO THINGS.** Often, the reason we hold on to things is from fear of being

in need. We believe a fear-based lie that if we need something or if we depend on someone, we're not adult enough to handle it alone. We're weak. But I believe we need to change our perspective on neediness! We are created to be in daily dependence on God; in fact, He created us to be driven to depend on Him. Stop making neediness negative.

3. **START SMALL.** We can quickly set ourselves up for failure when we focus only on the big picture. When we think about sharing, the tendency is to think about *all* we should share, or even more so, all we feel *obligated* to share. With that emphasis, we stop before we even start. Instead, start small. Give, as Ruth did, something simple. Pay it forward in the Starbucks line by covering the drink of the person behind you; volunteer one hour of time instead of an entire day. Take a baby step in sharing, then pause and reflect on the experience.

Yes, sharing is caring. But sharing is also blessing. No one said it better than wise ol' Solomon: "The generous will themselves be blessed, for they share their food with the poor" (Proverbs 22:9). Ruth shared what she had and was blessed in the end, not only with more food, but with her heart's desire: a family. Come on! That's what I call blessed!

CHAPTER 20

PEARLS OF [FRIENDSHIP] WISDOM

But Ruth replied, "Don't urge me to leave you or to turn back from you. Where you go I will go, and where you stay I will stay."

RUTH 1:16

In high school I saw an episode of *The Oprah Winfrey Show* where Oprah interviewed a group of long-standing friends who had stood together throughout the course of time. Each woman had neatly coiffed white hair and wore an identical pearl necklace on her clavicle. The women called themselves *The Pearls* because they were as tightly connected as a string of them—and they had sixty years of friendship to prove it.

Eyes glued to the television, I was mesmerized by how long they had been friends. Through college, moves, marriages, babies, divorces, and funerals, they had learned the art of friendship so beautifully that when the Queen of Talk Television read an article about them, she just *had* to bring them on her show. *The Pearls* explained how they'd met, what they loved about each other, and recounted funny stories they'd shared over six decades of friendship.

But the genuine ease on their faces after all those years was balanced by the deliberate effort they had obviously poured into *maintaining* their friendships. The truth came out through the telling of tales. Their bonds were forged and refined through a myriad of happy memories and fiery trials. From the loss of a job to the loss of a baby, from celebrating a wedding to mourning an affair, from buying a home to building a business, these women had seen it all and stayed with each other through thick and thin.

Watching their story unfold, I wondered: *Do I have friends like these? Am I this type of friend?*

In a world saturated by social media, where we can connect online with friends, fans, and followers, why is real-life community and in-person friendship important? I argue that community is important because it is the heart and nature of God. If the God of the universe placed an emphasis on the power of union and relationship by the creation of mankind, we can authoritatively say it's a priority to our Maker.

In Genesis 1, God made light and dark, and it was good. He created land and sea, and it was good. He created sea creatures and land creatures, and it was good. He created man—but in isolation, and God recognized that it was *not* good. Why? Because our Creator Himself exists in community. In Genesis 1:26, God says, "Let *us* make man in *our* image, after *our* likeness" (ESV, emphasis mine). The triune God—comprising God the Father, God the Son, and God the Holy Spirit—existed in relationship. As a remedy for Adam's aloneness, God created a friend and helper in the form of Eve.

But community and friendship aren't only found through marriage. From Moses and Aaron to Mary and Martha, friendship matters in countless ways. We are stronger together than when we are apart. King Solomon, in all his wisdom, knew the power of partnership when he said in Ecclesiastes 4:9–10, "Two are better than one, because they have a good return for their labor: If either of them falls down, one can help the other up. But pity anyone who falls and has no one to help them up."

Finding true friends isn't always easy. We need friends in our lives who are willing to go the hard yards with us, and in order to have them, we need also to *be* them.

> We need friends in our lives who are willing to go the hard yards with us, and in order to have them, we need also to *be* them.

Forever Friends

I met Melanie, Brianna, and Jennie when I was fourteen years old. Well, in the interest of full disclosure, my twin sister, Jasmine, met them first. I followed along and met them in our high school quad on a lunch break during freshman year, and we were always together after that. Like a mixed bag of LEGO pieces, we all looked different—black, white, Hispanic—but we clicked perfectly.

Whether on sports teams, in campus clubs, or planning school dances on student counsel, we did almost everything together. By the time senior year rolled around, we celebrated one another as we received our college acceptance letters. But what would happen to our close-knit group? Would our new lack of proximity—miles of highway and state lines between us—threaten our relationship? Could our friendship stand the test of time?

I remembered *The Pearls* and described in my journal the friendship qualities I thought they personified: courage in the midst of fear, strength in the midst of weakness, honesty in the midst of hurt, and commitment in the midst of chaos. Then, in the waning days of our last summer at home, I looked back at our four years of high school, and I feverishly scribbled down some of the powerful moments we had shared together.

I recalled the day Brianna, who balanced varsity sports and a part-time job, handed Jasmine an envelope of her hard-earned cash to buy a dress for our senior prom. Prior to that windfall, Jas nearly turned down her prospective date for lack of an appropriate dress, but instead was able to attend prom with the man who would eventually become her husband.

Then there was the midnight conversation in Jennie's powder-blue 1962 Chevy Impala, when I practically melted as my friends (in fiercest love) unrelentingly called me out on my aversion to conflict—a single event that has indelibly shaped my leadership to this day.

I remember when Melanie borrowed a car to drive out and watch me compete in the state speech competition, coaching, then calming, then comforting me when I lost in the final round.

We were always there for one another, cheering in sunny stadiums as Jennie and Bri shattered school records in softball and track and field, respectively. We celebrated and consoled each other through wins and losses in relationships, at soccer games, at cheer competitions, and in student body elections.

These memories were amazing, but I knew they alone wouldn't propel us into that next level of friendship I'd seen on *Oprah*. Still, I had to rely on them as fuel if I wanted to pursue long-term friendships. I had to bottle up all the courage, strength, honesty, and commitment of those four years and pour them into our future together.

After graduation, we all moved away for college. We emailed and texted frequently. We flew to visit each other and called during the late hours of the night to fill in the gaps distance and time created. In the years following high school and college, we fought for each other—when it was as natural as anything, and when it took everything we had.

When Bri's father tragically passed away, we dropped everything to travel to the funeral, weep with her, and hold her up in whatever ways we could.

When Melanie started her career, singing in LA clubs and at a big Orange County theme park, we showed up to fangirl in support. Now that she's playing mostly NFL stadiums with a world-renowned popstar, we show up and scream even louder.

When Jennie pitched her gold-medal-winning game at the Olympics, we all watched in our pajamas at ungodly hours of the night, sending our hearts and our prayers straight to the mound where she stood.

When Jasmine decided to adopt after twelve years of marriage, we surrounded her with love and support, vowing to be there as the long and difficult process unfolded.

When my laptop crashed two days before the deadline for my first book and I lost my entire final manuscript, Melanie spent a sleepless weekend helping me stitch it back together. Everyone rallied around me to celebrate the book launch.

We've welcomed husbands, stepchildren, and four new babies into the fold and still make time to connect one-on-one, and when we're really lucky, all together. We text almost daily with updates, prayer requests, encouragement, and emergency fashion shows.

I want to say we're friends because we were destined to be friends. But I'm not sure that would be entirely true. We are friends because we've remained determined to show up for each other, and that's made all the difference. Even when we've found ourselves screaming and yelling at each other, even when we've changed jobs and time zones, and even when we haven't agreed with or even liked each other, we've remained intent on loving each other no matter what. The relationship lasts because we are committed to staying the course, even when it seems littered with land mines. Please note: this will take so.much.work. You will fight, argue, cry, and possibly there will be moments when you don't even like each other. First, that's normal. Second, if you feel the relationship is worth fighting for, fight for it.

So what happens when the relationships can't or don't move forward? How can we end friendships well? Looking at the life of Ruth, Naomi, and Orpah on the road back to Bethlehem, we will see *how* and *when* relationships can transition.

Evaluate

Sometimes even very close relationships simply run their course. Our Old Testament friends faced this same challenge. Many theologians demonize Orpah for leaving Naomi in her greatest moment of need, but I don't think abandonment was at the heart of Orpah. Both Orpah and Ruth said, "We will go back with you to your people" (Ruth 1:9–10). Both women were *willing* to continue on the road to Bethlehem, but only one *wanted* to. Ruth pushed beyond being willing into a territory that forced her to declare she *wanted* to continue on the journey.

Before that declaration took place, though, Naomi initiated a conversation. Let's look at two ways that Naomi evaluated her relationship with her daughters-in-law during that talk.

1. Release

> *"May the LORD grant that each of you will find rest*
> *in the home of another husband." Then she kissed*
> *them goodbye and they wept aloud. (Ruth 1:9)*

Naomi released Ruth and Orpah (who, it's safe to assume, had become her friends during their time together in Moab). The release of a friend is a powerful act of maturity. When you feel like you can no longer give a friend what she needs in a season—like Naomi did for Orpah—don't be afraid to let her go. In like manner, don't be selfish and hold on to a person out of fear. People who feel trapped in a relationship often develop feelings of resentment and anger toward a friend who hasn't released them to grow up or move on.

In chapter one of Ruth, Naomi acknowledged she had nothing left to offer Ruth and Orpah. Acknowledging there was no hope of a future or family for herself, Naomi demonstrated self-awareness and bravely admitted her season of life. In doing so, she gave Ruth and Orpah the option to leave.

Being a self-aware friend and admitting the season you are in is another sign of maturity. As hard as it is, admitting there is a problem is the first step to gaining clarity on how to move forward, even if that means releasing a friend from the relationship.

2. Reality

> But Naomi said, "Return home, my daughters.
> Why would you come with me?" (Ruth 1:11)

The life Naomi once lived with her daughters-in-law was gone. Reality had sunk in. I can picture Naomi saying, "The home we lived in? My son, the love of your life? My husband who provided for us? The life we once lived? They're gone. I have nothing to give you." The things that once tied them together no longer existed.

Naomi knew her daughters-in-law didn't owe her anything. Ruth and Orpah had pledged commitments to her sons, and legally, there was no binding contract between them once those sons died. The reality was that Naomi's friendship with Ruth and Orpah was a friendship by association. Without her sons, what relationship did Naomi *really* have with her daughters-in-law?

If a friendship is formed as a by-product of another friendship or situation, and something changes (your married friends get divorced, a friend has a falling out with a mutual friend, the contract job where you met a friend terminates, etc.), there might be a time when you evaluate whether a relationship should continue. It might be time for a reality check.

End of the Road

The painful truth is that some friendships are seasonal. It doesn't mean they were fake, phony, or fraudulent. It simply means those friends were in our lives for a reason and a season. We can walk away feeling bitter because we invested time and energy into someone who is no longer our friend OR we can choose to feel blessed because of all the wonderful things that came from that relationship. Either way, it's important to ask ourselves, *Did that friend need to be released? Am I aware of the reality of this situation?*

Sometimes a relationship can run its course and we need to let go. *This is okay.* It doesn't mean that you were bad or that your friend was bad. The end of your friendship means the season of being friends is over.

> Sometimes a relationship can run its course and we need to let go. *This is okay.*

This might simply be proximity. They moved, or you moved, and distance over time has limited your conversations and commonalities. The girls' nights and coffee dates are no longer possible, and distance between you has pulled your friendship apart. Is it time to face reality and release your friend?

When I got married and moved from Los Angeles to Orange County, I suddenly discovered a world of obstacles between me and some of my closest friends. Nothing bad happened, but distance made it feel like we needed military precision to coordinate calendars. Two of my friends remained connected and intentional. They were incredibly busy as well, so they understood the craziness of life and didn't need constant contact or time.

These friends—Jeanette and Diane—are the most low-maintenance friends I have. We give huge amounts of grace to Jeanette because she is a working mother of three children and passionate about maintaining a healthy marriage. We know her family comes first. We give huge amounts of grace to Diane because she is a successful business owner who travels extensively with her husband. We don't do phone calls, we don't do weekly hangouts, and we often don't even know what part of the nation the others are in, but we do know we love each other and vow to see each other a couple of times a year. The clarity and realistic expectations we have about our relationship make it easy to connect on those rare occasions when we're able to, and to pick up right where we left off.

However, not all relationships transition this easily. Sometimes there is a bigger issue that causes a wedge or division to fracture the friendship. I intimately know the pain of walking through this. Several years ago, I met an awesome woman and instantly knew we'd be great friends. True to my instinct, we shared passions, similar family dynamics, and loved many of the same things. For years we traveled together, dreamed together, and shared life together. Our families were intimately connected, and she was the closest person I confided in.

But over time, insecurity and overall distrust wedged their way into our hearts, and a ten-year relationship ended in the most painful way. The toughest part of it all wasn't that there was an issue we couldn't fix or a problem we had yet to clarify. It was simply me. She didn't like the person I had become.

For months I was angry—seething over the fact that she hadn't simply rejected our friendship, she had rejected me for an unknown, unstated reason.

She said some very hurtful things during the last few months of our relationship, but after months of praying and meeting with a trusted mentor who encouraged me to learn from this, I began to heal. Part of that process involved confronting the reality of what my friend had said. It took me a while to get it, but as I began to journal some of her grievances with me, I realized (as hard as it was to admit) I had really played a bigger part in the ending of our friendship than I'd thought.

Sadly, we never recovered, and we aren't friends today. That doesn't mean we will never be friends, but it does mean I have learned from my mistakes as a friend and believe I am a better person because of that relationship.

If you feel a friendship has run its course, do not ignore the signs or sweep them under the rug. If we avoid conflict or hard conversations, it will limit our maturity and cause greater pain in the future. Be a grown woman and face conflict valiantly. Seek clarity while there is still time for conversation to be had. Otherwise, greater hurt and confusion can cause distrust and fear to negatively affect future friendships.

How to Find Friends

So after all this talk about friends, how do we actually find friends who will go the distance with us? What should we be looking for when it comes to friendship? Better yet, how can we BE the kind of friend we would want in our own life?

Here is a quick list à la the life of Ruth on how to be the friend we'd want to have:

- Listen to and heed good counsel from a friend (Ruth 3:5).
- Care and cry with friends during moments of grief (Ruth 1:9).
- Eat meals together (and bring home leftovers to share) (Ruth 2:18).

- Support each other emotionally (and even financially within means) during crisis moments (Ruth 1:14, 2:2).
- Allow each other the opportunity to help out with family needs (Ruth 4:16).
- Celebrate together when God blesses you (Ruth 4:13–17).

Do a quick friend check. Do you embody these attributes? Is there someone you're in community with who exemplifies those qualities? What would it look like to invest in her and see if a deeper friendship forms?

Finding and making friends isn't always easy. But when we intentionally evaluate what season we are in, like Naomi, we can release the Orpahs in our lives while discovering who our Ruths will be. Don't be afraid to put yourself out there. Remember, if you want someone to go the hard yards for you, you must be willing to go the hard yards for her.

Now take these pearls of wisdom I've given you and string them together to make your own necklace. You got this!

JESUS ON FRIENDSHIP

In His three and a half years of documented ministry work, Jesus became friends with His disciples. A man surrounded daily by hundreds and even thousands of people used wisdom to decipher who to bring into His personal and private space.

We live in a world where we use social media language like *followers* (Twitter and Instagram), and *fans* and *friends* (Facebook). Let's see how Jesus dealt with relationships using these convenient terms and the imagery of concentric circles.

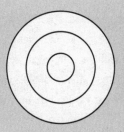

Fans: The Outer Circle

Fans had the least access to Jesus. They watched from afar, and if they were healed or provided with lunch, they loved Him. They were the ones who sang, "Hosanna, hosanna," as Jesus entered Jerusalem on the back of a donkey while they waved palm leaves. And they were the same ones who yelled, "Crucify Him!" on Good Friday. Fans are fickle and can turn their backs on their supposed friends without thinking twice.

Though we might not be able to resonate with fans like the ones Jesus had, there will be people who come into our lives with the hope of achieving some personal gain—networking, status, access to your circle, and more. Be careful in bringing them too close. Time is a great vetting process. In time, character, loyalty, and trust are built. Before getting too close to someone, make sure you know their intentions and spend time fostering the potential friendship.

Followers: The Middle Circle

Jesus invited several men to follow Him, and they became His disciples. Day in and day out, they did life together. From serving people food to surviving a storm, these men were by Jesus's side during His ministry on earth. Trusted, available, and loyal, this motley gang of ragamuffins became Jesus's crew. Not only did the disciples *follow* Jesus, these men are referred to as His friends in John 15:15: "I no longer call you servants, because a servant does not know his master's business. Instead, I have called you friends." Together they changed the world.

We, too, will live with people in community. We will share meals together and dream of the future together. We spend so much time with these people because we trust them. Though we won't always get along and may come from different backgrounds, our shared beliefs and the call on our lives will unite us in community. This community may be found in our neighborhood, church, or even through ministry. Invest in this community, and you might just be surprised at the ways you can follow in the footsteps of Jesus and change those around you.

Friends: The Inner Circle

Of the twelve disciples with whom Jesus lived and ministered, there were three men He brought into His personal world. Peter, James, and John were the closest to Jesus and witnessed some of His most painful and powerful moments. When Jesus was about to face crucifixion, He invited Peter, James, and John to join Him and pray in the Garden of Gethsemane. When Jesus was on the Mount of Transfiguration, His three amigos were right by His side. These men proved to be the closest and most trusted friends of Jesus.

A trusted inner circle will take time to build. But these friendships will involve intimate access to the most painful and powerful moments of your lives. It will be worth it.

CHAPTER 21

DO THE HARD WORK

So she went out, entered a field and began to glean behind the harvesters.

RUTH 2:3

I read the top of her résumé and raised a brow as I noticed the uniqueness of her name. *Chelsie, with an "ie."* Sure, the name was common enough, but its spelling was unusual. And while her résumé didn't include a whole lot to make it stand out from the stack on my desk, *Chelsie* possessed something different. We sat across from each other at a white circular table in a small office. She was poised and seemed completely prepared to answer all my questions. I, on the other hand, was ready to go full-on Anna Wintour from *Vogue* and pick her apart. A good number of people had applied to volunteer with me for a good number of reasons, but I was wary of taking the time to train an intern. I just wanted to get back to work.

After a string of flighty college students showing up late with haphazard work ethics and complicated emotions, I was more than ready to stop accepting applications. (Maybe someday I'll be bold enough to tell you about the time I almost strangled one. But that's a story for another day.) But I was running myself completely ragged trying to do everything on my own. The whole office knew it and insisted I find someone to help.

As I spoke with Chelsie, I noticed her competitive fire when she talked about her collegiate basketball career. Puzzled as to why someone with her background would want to intern at an NGO, I pressed her for answers and was pleasantly surprised by her transparency. Chelsie was very honest about what she was after.

"I've never seen a Christian woman preach like you or do what you're doing in the social justice space," she said. "I'm looking for a mentor because I think I might be called to ministry. Maybe more importantly, though, I want to keep you from continuing to be a hot mess."

I should have been offended, but instead I laughed. I laughed because it was *funny*, and I laughed because it was *true*.

Before that afternoon in my office, Chelsie and I had connected briefly online. She'd heard me speak at Biola University and reached out on social media with a very sweet post. I replied, thanking her for attending chapel. She, in turn, asked if I offered any internships. Still in the throes of post-traumatic stress from my previous intern disaster (you remember, the gal I almost strangled), I wished her the best with my most gracious "thanks, but no thanks."

If you don't follow me on social media, you might not know how embarrassingly real I keep my accounts. I openly share my myriad mix-ups because it's hilarious to me that God has seen fit to continually use a mess like me. But now, with every mistake I made and posted online, Chelsie was there to reply.

When I booked a flight to the wrong city and posted about it on Facebook, she jokingly commented, "Do you need an intern?" I thanked her but said no.

A few weeks later, I posted on Twitter that I'd accidentally taken the wrong suitcase from the baggage carousel at Dallas International. Upon opening it at my hotel, I realized my mistake when I discovered a large man's underthings. Chelsie again commented: "Are you *sure* you don't need an intern?"

I *didn't* need an intern. Interns, in all my experience with them, had always proved to be more hindrance than help. But with extensive travel approaching, deadlines at work, and creative projects piling up, I knew I needed *something*.

I decided I'd have to ignore every (very reasonable) reason I had *not* to meet with her, and skeptically asked Chelsie to send me her résumé. Even then, though, I didn't make it easy. I gave her the absolute tiniest of timeframes to come in for an interview. In hindsight, it shouldn't have surprised me at all that within the hour, she had responded accommodatingly and agreed to my absurdly narrow terms.

Unbeknownst to me at the time, Chelsie had to skip class and brave an hour of traffic just to ensure she would arrive on time. (Note: I'm not advocating ditching classes, but when I found out, I was definitely impressed by Chelsie's chutzpa.) Prompt and self-possessed, she softened me with her zeal and humility; zeal to do the difficult and often thankless work of an intern at an underfunded NGO, and humility in recognizing she had much to learn.

When I asked if there were any particular duties she was hoping to take on in this role, a serious look came over her face. "Anything," she replied with sincerity. "I will do anything I have to in order to fulfill my role with excellence."

It was as if the words *anything* and *excellence* were the magic pills that finally wiped my memory of the harrowing intern dramas from my past. Chelsie's willingness to do and bring her best let me know I'd finally met the girl I needed.

Work Like Ruth

Any good boss will pick a team carefully. Like Boaz, I want to ensure the people I'm working alongside are trustworthy, hardworking, and honest—just like Ruth.

Boaz asked the overseer of his harvesters, "Who does that young woman belong to?"

The overseer replied, "She is the Moabite who came back from Moab with Naomi. She said, 'Please let me glean and gather among the sheaves behind the harvesters.' She came into the field and has remained here from morning till now, except for a short rest in the shelter." (Ruth 2:5–7)

Ruth's job was a matter of life and death. She wasn't interning to gain experience; she was working so she could provide for her family. Nonetheless, when we consider this piece of her story, there are still some amazing lessons we can learn from her and apply to the way we enter the workforce.

So she went out, entered a field and began to glean behind the harvesters. (Ruth 2:3)

1. So she went out . . .

Heading into the professional world might be intimidating. But becoming an adult requires you to take steps toward your goals, in spite of any fear and uncertainty. Ruth didn't know anyone in Bethlehem. However, she knew her livelihood depended on her ability to provide for herself and for Naomi. So she went out into the world and got to work.

As with any leap of faith, there is the possibility of rejection. But with nothing ventured, there is nothing gained. Chelsie reached out three times before I agreed to meet with her. And I rejected her every time! Did my rejection stop her from putting herself out there? No. And rejection shouldn't stop you from chasing after what you want.

As Ruth stepped out to work in the morning, she knew that in order to survive tomorrow, she had to work today. Just as *she went out*, we must also put ourselves out in the world and find work.

2. . . . entered a field . . .

Pause and take note that Ruth didn't roll into Bethlehem and act like she owned the place. She didn't show up and tell people what to do or where to go. She was aware that she was starting at square one, with nothing. How far do you imagine she'd have gotten with an air of entitlement, acting like it was her right to start at the management level or claim a top-dollar paycheck?

The field she entered belonged to Boaz, not to her. Similarly, our offices and places of employment most likely aren't ours, either. When we enter someone else's space, we must respect it and recognize our roles. Just as Boaz selected and allowed people to work for him, our employers have done the same for us. Respect your field and enter it with humility.

3. . . . began to glean . . .

Unless you were raised on a farm or have agricultural experience, the word *glean*, as it's used here, might not be in your vocabulary.

Gleaning is the act of collecting leftover crops from farmers' fields after they have been harvested. Gleaning in a modern context is a term meaning "to collect gradually and bit by bit."

Though most of us don't work in *actual* fields, we can apply the gleaning principle to our lives. Wherever you work, you have the opportunity to *glean* knowledge, wisdom, and insight from your trainers,

Don't ever think that the tasks you do are too small to provide you with opportunities to learn.

bosses, and coworkers. Don't ever think that the tasks you do are too small to provide you with opportunities to learn.

4. . . . behind the harvesters.

For many of my young friends, this concept is a jagged little pill to swallow. Especially in America, where pushing boundaries, racing to win, and fighting for first place is what we're taught to do. But there are valuable lessons we will surely miss if we don't look to the people who paved the path we get to walk on.

Ruth recognized that her role was to stay behind the harvesters. These were trained farmers who knew what they were doing. The Bible doesn't mention what kind of work Ruth might have done in Moab. She may never have been on a farm before. But for all we know, she might also have been the female Old MacDonald. What we can be sure of is that she needed a job when she arrived in Bethlehem, so she humbled herself and followed the harvesters.

When I entered the workforce at the age of twenty-two, I was certain I would be a game changer—as if four years of undergrad had taught me everything I could possibly need to know (it was all *very* un-Ruthlike of me). Opinionated and eager, I found myself tripping over my ego and wondering why no one cared what I had to say. Thankfully, a staff member named Joe pulled me aside one day and gently said, "Bianca, your greatest strength is your greatest weakness. You're full of big ideas, but truthfully, you've never executed any of them. You need to be patient and give people a chance to learn to trust you. Get some wins on the board, stay humble, do the work, and in time, people will start to listen. Otherwise, you're just the new kid who thinks she knows it all."

That was a jagged little pill for me to swallow. But Joe knew what he was talking about. I apologized to some coworkers, made lunch appointments to learn from staff, and met with Joe every quarter to assess what improvements he had seen in my work, as well as in my willingness to learn from others. Trust me on this one. It's way less embarrassing not to have to learn this the hard way.

Do the Hard Work

In his 2008 book *Outliers*, Malcolm Gladwell writes, "Ten thousand hours is the magic number of greatness . . . in an incredible number of fields . . . you need to have practiced, to have apprenticed, for ten thousand hours before you get good."[1] His examples include Steve Jobs, who began coding as a teenager, and the Beatles, a band that paid its dues at many an eight-hour club gig, long before the American Invasion. "People aren't born geniuses," Gladwell continues, "they get there through repeated effort."[2] But if these five geniuses hadn't seized opportunities to practice early and often, I wouldn't be typing this sentence from my MacBook, and rock and roll music would have never been the same.

Hard work is just that: *hard*. So what does excellence look like day to day?

- If you're a teacher, it's lesson planning and teaching children who aren't yours.
- If you're a mother, it's loving and caretaking selflessly (and sometimes without gratitude).
- If you're a student, it's going to class, turning in assignments, and applying yourself.
- If you're in an entry-level job at a corporation, it's showing up on time, caring about your work, and going the distance on all projects.

If Chelsie hadn't interned with me, I still believe she would have been destined for great things. But in her willingness to commit to hard work and glean from those who'd gone before her, she was able to capitalize on some amazing opportunities. Over the years, Chelsie and I have traveled extensively throughout the United States and as far away as Mexico, Great Britain, Israel, and Italy. What's more, she's stepped out on her own to work with the Women's National Basketball Association (WNBA), has been a guest lecturer at the university level, and pioneered the first women's Bible study on her former college campus. Chelsie went from being an intern to being a part-time team member, and is now working in full-time ministry. God continues to bless her efforts because of the work she is always willing to do.

Are there times when working in someone else's field is hard? Yes. Are there moments when you are tired and want to quit? Absolutely. But if the Lord has called you to that field, work diligently toward excellence. Do it for ten thousand hours.

THOUGHTS FROM A THERAPIST

Dr. Deb on Character

Boaz gives us the best example of what a boss really notices in an employee and what we tend to lose sight of in the job application process—*character*. It's all too easy for us to focus heavily on the knowledge and skills part of a job's requirements when considering what it takes to succeed and as the essential way to impress the boss. We rarely look beyond those elements and focus on our dispositions, but Boaz did. He wasn't impressed with Ruth's skills at gleaning or her knowledge of farming. He took notice of her demeanor—she was humble, dedicated, and consistent. It was her character that counted.

One of the most valuable character traits you can display as an employee is openness and receptivity to feedback. If you want to consistently impress the boss, demonstrate a posture that says, "I'm listening to understand what you're saying, what the need is, and what I can do to put your feedback into action."

Good employers don't expect their employees to be perfect. They expect them to work hard and receive insight and critical evaluation with a willingness to consider the benefits and growth that feedback can bring.

Unfortunately, unchecked attitudes in critical conversations often lead to unintentional (or maybe intentional!) defensiveness. You might think that statements such as "I did it that way because I thought it would be better" or "I didn't have time to get everything done" show the boss you were trying your best or didn't do something on purpose. However, those types of responses usually just come across as justifications. They end up sending the message that you aren't really listening to or invested in what's being communicated to you. Nothing aggravates a boss more than an employee that "listens" to respond versus listens to understand.

Critical feedback is uncomfortable. It can touch on our deepest insecurities and make us squirm, question our abilities, and face intense feelings of anxiety and frustration. But think about the fact that even the most belligerent of bosses is probably not giving you feedback simply to make your life miserable or cut you down to size (and if that's really the case, it's time to start looking for a new job!). It's more likely that their main purpose is helping you accomplish the responsibilities you've been given in the way that's expected.

If you want to set yourself up for success in the work that you do, be intentional in committing to your character just as much, if not more, than your skill set. The Boaz-bosses of the world will take notice.

CHAPTER 22

THIS IS JUST A SEASON

And [Ruth] lived with her mother-in-law.
RUTH 2:23

Bat mitzvah. Sweet sixteen. Quinceañera. Every culture has rites of passage which signify crossing the threshold from childhood into adulthood. Whether it's a Latin American spiritual presentation like in a quinceañera at fifteen or a Kenyan community event celebrating a boy becoming a man at thirteen, the line of demarcation clearly grants someone access to sit at the adult table of life. Gone are the kiddy chairs and plastic plates; you are a grown adult.

For many, adulthood in the West is idealized, unclear, and difficult to define. Leading sociologists have determined that certain characteristics of adolescence—not working a full-time job, living at home, and demonstrating an aversion to taking responsibility—now extend late into people's twenties and even early thirties. One psychologist coined the term *emerging adulthood* for the previously uncharacterized phase of life between eighteen and twenty-five.[1]

And though I believe the research, and did, in fact, find myself working part-time and living at home in my twenties, I wish someone would've pulled me aside and whispered, *This is only for a season.*

At twenty-four, I was mostly unemployed in spite of a bachelor's degree, living rent-free with my parents, and as single as a one-dollar bill. I made ends meet by cleaning offices, babysitting, and doing random editing jobs while stiff-arming Sallie Mae as she tried to collect on my college loan payments. During that season, *Time* magazine came out with a revealing study about eighteen- to thirty-year-olds who were emerging into adult society ill-equipped and unemployed.

I was sitting on my parents' couch in my parents' house, eating food my parents paid for while reading a magazine subscription that wasn't mine. As the report droned on about the lack of integrity in my generation, I dropped the magazine over my face and cried out, "I'M A LOSER!"

The truth: I wasn't a loser. I was in a period of transition. If you find yourself living in a situation you never imagined for yourself, give yourself a break and acknowledge it's just for a season. (Unless, of course, you're in a situation where you are perpetuating your circumstances with a series of poor decisions—no job, dropped out of school, stoner who loves to party, poor manager of finances who has plenty of credit debt—you get the picture. If this is you, please know that without serious change, your *season* will eventually become a *lifetime* of suck.)

Recent research from the United States Census Bureau says that 36 percent of adults still live at home with their parents.[2] As with Ruth, events beyond our control will force us to make decisions. But before you lament and label yourself a loser, let's take a look at Ruth's life and why she was living with her mother-in-law:

- Ruth wasn't married.
- Ruth didn't have a job.
- Ruth was in a new city and didn't know anyone.

- Ruth didn't have anyone in her life she could trust other than Naomi.

I was so quick to highlight my failures that I missed key personal challenges and societal changes that forced me to make the decisions I did (like live at home and feel like a leech):

- The year I graduated college was the beginning of the second worst economic depression in US history since the Great Depression.
- My mother was going through chemotherapy and I was asked to help out.
- I wasn't married.
- I couldn't find a job (and I had been rejected by three different *internships* where I would have worked for free!).

It's important to note the factors surrounding your life. As insignificant as one may seem, collaboratively they can shape our entire outlook on self, goals, ambition, and success. In Dr. Jeffrey Arnett's groundbreaking book, *Emerging Adulthood*, he takes a look at where we are as a society in order to help guide the next generation as they emerge into adulthood:

MORE EDUCATION. According to Dr. Arnett, many emerging adults will go to college or graduate school as a way to stall adulthood. I was one of them. While sitting on my parents' couch, crying about being a loser, I decided to go to graduate school. Even with an impressive résumé and 3.84 GPA, I couldn't find a job. So I went to grad school to delay growing up and defer my loan payments.

THE DEMAND FOR JOBS IN THE UNITED STATES IS INCREASINGLY COMPETITIVE. Seventy-five percent of college students graduate without a job lined up. So, like I did, they jump on board the grad school bus for another two to four years of education. Sociologists suggest going back to school is now seen as a viable and worthwhile detour from adulthood. Living with a flexible schedule and surviving on school loans feels like a better option than working forty hours a week.

PEOPLE ARE GETTING MARRIED LATER IN LIFE. This is quite possibly the most important factor facing emerging adults. Fifty years ago, the average age someone got married was twenty years old. In 2017, the average marrying age was between twenty-eight and thirty—and it's still rising! This is important to note because marriage directly affects the identity formation of emerging adults. Marriage in the past has been a clear indicator of adulthood and created a natural shift in the parent-child relationship.

According to Dr. Arnett, getting married at a young age used to provide people with committed partners to help them navigate life. He notes, "Today, emerging adults don't have this kind of partnership; instead they rely more on their parents."[3]

Perhaps because of my fear of commitment, I didn't get married until I was thirty years old. When my husband, Matt, and I returned from our honeymoon, I sat on our bed and felt the weight of adulthood. I knew my season had changed, and I felt both excited (my life was in a new season) and scared (I had to be responsible and start paying rent again)!

SEX IS ENGAGED DIFFERENTLY. Back in the day, if we wanted to have sex, a large contingent of American culture demanded someone put a ring on it. Sex was a sign of maturity, responsibility, and marital commitment. But more and more, it's regarded merely as an act of personal enjoyment and an expression of individual freedom.

Where did the concept of sex within marriage come from? The Bible. Sex was a gift reserved only for those who had made a covenant. However, culture has removed the exclusivity and priority of marriage and encouraged men to follow suit with Peter Pan and women to follow suit with Pippi Longstocking: have fun and don't grow up.

No matter what challenges you have faced in transitioning to adulthood, remember that this season isn't forever. Maybe you are living at home with your parents. Maybe your home is a cramped apartment with thin walls and dated shag carpet. Maybe you share a bedroom with a roommate or two. Maybe you are recently divorced and bunking on a friend's couch because you have nowhere to go. Factors beyond your control may have precluded you from feeling like a successful, grown woman. Don't worry! This is just for a season.

> Don't waste the season of life you are in because you are anxious for the season to come.

The underlying narrative of Ruth's story—and our stories—is that no season is forever. Ruth was in a season where she was living with Naomi and helping her, just as I found myself moving back home and helping my family during illness (and personal job-lessness). Don't waste the season of life you are in because you are anxious for the season to come. Ruth didn't stay there, I didn't stay there, and you won't stay where you are, either.

CHAPTER 23

WERK, WERK, WERK

"She said, 'Please let me glean and gather among the sheaves behind the harvesters.' She came into the field and has remained here from morning till now, except for a short rest in the shelter."

RUTH 2:7

Every morning Kristen was the first to arrive at the office. With her coffee mug placed neatly on her desk, she plugged in her earphones and worked diligently—day after day, week after week, and month after month. Though all the employees at A21 headquarters were millennials, twenty-year-old Kristen was the youngest by far. A fair-skinned, blue-eyed Michigan native, Kristen was impressively dedicated to her job, making a regular practice of working overtime and always finding time to help me on projects, edit briefs, and proof new proposals.

Kristen (and the team at A21) is the reason I wildly resent the way the media portrays millennials. *Lazy*, *entitled*, and *privileged* are only some of the words critics use to describe the work ethic of Generation Y. Other pejorative terms used in identifying this group include *snowflake* (based on the concept that millennials see themselves as special and unique), *gen me* (based on the concept of individual selfishness), and the *Peter Pan generation* (based on the concept of *adultescence* and a desire to never grow up).

Having spent six years at A21, surrounded by talented, dedicated, hardworking next-generation freedom fighters ceaselessly working to abolish slavery, I felt like the world was selling me a lie.

But as it's been said, stereotypes are based on a preponderance of truth. It would be foolish of me to ignore that research supports the idea that millennials have a lower work ethic than previous generations. For example, the nationally recognized Monitoring the Future project has surveyed half a million high school seniors since 1976. Here's how three generations answered three questions related to work ethic:[1]

	Baby Boomers	Generation X	Millennials
Don't want to work hard	26%	30%	38%
Willing to work overtime	59%	56%	40%
If had enough money would not want to work	22%	26%	31%

While I recognize that the data shows a lower desire to work among the millennial generation, I also subscribe to the school of thought that if you don't like the story, you can change the narrative. (Thanks, Don Draper, for your marketing genius!)

Ruth had labels and stereotypes working against her, much the way Kristen and others like her do today. But Ruth decidedly shattered any expectations that she was going to beg for handouts, do subpar work, or quit early. Ruth developed a shining reputation on the job built solely by her own dedicated effort.

The moment Ruth arrived in Bethlehem, she began to look for work. There was no time for pity parties. She needed to find a way to survive.

So Ruth **gleaned** in the field until evening. Then she **threshed** the barley she had gathered, and it amounted to about an **ephah**. (Ruth 2:17)

In one short verse we learn how dedicated she was to earning a living, and I believe we can learn from Ruth's work ethic. Let's break that down.

Ruth Gleaned Until Evening

Manual labor wasn't beneath Ruth. Backbreaking fieldwork wasn't offensive to her. She knew that if she didn't work, she didn't eat, so she worked until evening. In other words, Ruth worked overtime.

When the harvest is ready—or in our case, when work is due—we must be willing to go the extra mile, finish the project, and maximize our opportunities to gain the highest yield for our efforts.

Werk, girl.

Ruth Threshed Barley

Employees at *Boaz Barley Enterprises* would usually be responsible for individual tasks. That is to say, some workers would glean, some would gather, some would thresh, some would store the grain. But our role model, Ruth, DID IT ALL. After gleaning and gathering (two exhausting tasks), she made her way to the threshing floor to winnow the barley as well. Ruth was a one-woman show all on her own.

Be like Ruth—a woman who shows up to work as the can-do, make-it-work problem solver! You can always do more than the minimum which is required of you. You can take on a few extra responsibilities or pitch a great idea. Be the woman who's willing to sell that idea and see it through to completion.

Werk, girl.

Ruth Earned an Ephah

No one gave Ruth a free meal. She worked hard for her money! A full day of labor amounted to almost forty pounds of barley. (Note: the Hebrew weight referred to as an *ephah* is roughly five gallons, which weighs roughly forty pounds.[2] You're welcome.) Ruth worked all day and walked home carrying FORTY POUNDS of grain. This woman was in total beast mode and puts CrossFit fanatics to shame.

If Ruth wasn't afraid of sweat and hard work, we shouldn't be afraid to apply a little elbow grease and grit. Forget your aversion to sweat or manual labor because hard work almost always requires it. If we are committed to our work and believe it's almost harvest season (read: time to reap our rewards), then one day it will be. And we will be ready. Just like Proverbs says, "Those who work their land will have abundant food, but those who chase fantasies have no sense" (12:11).

Werk, girl.

For Kristen, the hours she invested and the commitment to excellence she exhibited paid off in her own ephah of barley. At the ripe age of twenty-seven, Kristen became a global director for A21 and the youngest staff member to establish the organization's presence in one of the most influential cities in America: Washington, DC. Statistics, labels, and stereotypes aside, Kristen wrote her own narrative and worked like it was harvest season.

So how can we break the mold? How can we transform the stereotypes people place on us? How can we rewrite the narrative that calls us a generation of selfish, lazy, overgrown kids? It's simple. Do the opposite of what people negatively assume we'll do.

If you struggle with punctuality, set your clock ahead so you arrive on time. If you feel disorganized, consider a digital management tool or Google calendar that syncs to your phone so you always have access to your schedule. If you sense your boss struggles to communicate with you, initiate a meeting to establish communication preferences or ways to better improve your working relationship. If this seems out of reach, ask your mentor what they suggest. The term *millennial* doesn't have to define you. You are allowed to reappropriate that label. You are allowed to write your own narrative—or to rewrite the one people have crafted on your behalf.

Werk, werk, werk. Then carry your barley home like a boss.

CHAPTER 24

REDEMPTION AND LEGACY

So Boaz took Ruth and she became his wife. When he made love to her, the LORD enabled her to conceive, and she gave birth to a son.

This, then, is the family line of Perez:
Perez was the father of Hezron,
Hezron the father of Ram,
Ram the father of Amminadab,
Amminadab the father of Nahshon,
Nahshon the father of Salmon,
Salmon the father of Boaz,
Boaz the father of Obed,
Obed the father of Jesse,
and Jesse the father of David.
RUTH 4:13, 18–22

Mildred Rodriguez sat in her beige Volkswagen Beetle and hid the tears streaming down her face behind her long red hair. Alone and terrified, she knew she had lost two people that day: her boyfriend and their unborn baby. Though she loved her boyfriend, starting a family out of wedlock at twenty-one years old wasn't something she had planned. Against her boyfriend's wishes, she walked into an abortion facility. She walked out feeling more alone than she had ever been before.

Reeling from her painful decision, Mildred fell into a spiral of depression. Her boyfriend resented her because of her decision and broke up with her shortly thereafter. The alcohol in which Mildred used to find comfort now just made her ill. The friends she had hung out with and the parties that once filled her weekends with adventures suddenly felt as hollow and empty as her womb. She'd lost even more than her relationship and her child; she'd lost herself.

What do you do when dreams are broken and nothing feels salvageable? Whether by our own choices, or because of circumstances out of our control, we will have moments when we feel like all hope is gone and redemption—the action of being saved from our sin—is impossible.

But listen closely: redemption is never out of reach.

> **Redemption is never out of reach.**

The theme of redemption is addressed in 150 texts of Scripture. Finding its context in the social, legal, and religious customs of the ancient world, redemption (*gaal* in Hebrew) includes the idea of being released from a bond or debt, being set free from captivity or slavery, or buying back something lost or sold. This is why Isaiah refers to God as our Redeemer who said, "Do not fear, for I have redeemed you; I have called you by name; you are Mine!" (Isaiah 43:1 NASB). God has paid the debt of our mistakes, freed us from the slavery of sin, and bought us back into His freedom.

Though physical slavery isn't likely something you have dealt with, we have a Redeemer who can rescue and redeem us from all forms of emotional, spiritual, and psychological bondage. The alcohol addiction in your past? God can redeem it. The broken heart from being abandoned? God can redeem it. The abuse you endured at the hands of another? God can redeem it. The bankruptcy and the credit card debt you piled up while trying to find significance? God can redeem it. Not only does God forgive our sins, but He goes even further and brings good out of life's most painful moments (Romans 8:28).

Redemption isn't easy, and it's not always quick. But we have a God who desires to right all wrongs—to buy back the narrative and redeem even the most painful story. Our Redeemer has rescued us from our sin, shame, and selfishness (Isaiah 47:4). Therefore, nothing is beyond the reach of the hand of our great God.

Throughout the pages of Ruth's story, we discovered a woman who lost everything and whose life was as barren as the landscape from Moab to Bethlehem. But God redeemed her story—He righted all wrongs, forgave all sins—and turned her life around.

Redemption Is Real

Ruth was a woman who had nothing and gave up everything. Boaz was a man who gave everything and expected nothing. Together they made a decision to commit their lives to each other and built a future that—as we will uncover—affects our faith, even today.

In Ruth 4:13 we read about the wedding of Ruthie and Bo. This wedding was the beautiful turning point in the story of Ruth's life. The new-to-town, barren widow with the widowed mother-in-law stood in front of her new community and married the man who had chosen her. And though this was incredibly romantic, it was extremely significant, too. Marrying Boaz—a Jew—officially made Ruth part of the Israel community (which, for a Moabite, was pretty close to miraculous!).

For students of the Bible and even some theologians, the fact that Ruth was brought into Israelite life is problematic. Why? Because according to Mosaic law in Deuteronomy 23:3, no Moabite could be admitted into the covenant community. To talk about redemption and not talk about *our* lives as outsiders would be tragic. We aren't Ruth, but most of us have felt outside the community of God at some point. Maybe we're like Ruth, who never heard about the one true God. Maybe we're a bit more like Naomi, who left the community of God's people in spite of how others might've scoffed or questioned her family's decision.

In Genesis 17 we are told that anyone—regardless of race, gender, or ethnicity—who became a believer in Yahweh could become an Israelite. And on the road to Bethlehem, that was Ruth's exact declaration (Ruth 1:16). This is such a wonderful reminder for us that it doesn't matter where we've come from (perhaps you've had some Moab party days, days when you were devastated and alone, days when you were starving). What matters is where we are going (Bethlehem, the house of bread).

Because Naomi and Ruth were poor, widowed, and alone, they needed a redeemer. In their case this meant a near relative who was willing and able to restore and reclaim them. Enter Boaz.

> Then Boaz announced to the elders and all the people, "Today you are witnesses that I have bought from Naomi all the property of Elimelek, Kilion and Mahlon. I have also acquired Ruth the Moabite, Mahlon's widow, as my wife, in order to maintain the name of the dead with his property, so that his name will not disappear from among his family or from his hometown. Today you are witnesses!" (Ruth 4:9–10)

Boaz stepped up and demonstrated real life redemption. When a closer relative to Naomi refused to do the job (Ruth 4:1–8), Boaz purchased land from Naomi and absorbed not only the land but also the women as his responsibility. In the words of the '90s hip-hop group Salt-N-Pepa, "What a man! What a man! What a man! What a mighty good man! He's a mighty, mighty good man!"

It is for this reason that Charles Spurgeon calls Jesus Christ "our great and glorious Boaz"! From Bethlehem, the house of bread, comes Jesus, the bread of life. Jesus is similar yet superior to Boaz. As Boaz redeemed Ruth and rescued her, Jesus—our great and glorious Redeemer—has rescued us. All you have to do is claim that God is your God, His people are your people, where He goes you will go, and nothing will separate you from Him.

Jesus was willing and able to redeem humanity, to save us from our sin, to claim us as His chosen, and to promise us a life under the protection of His wings. Whether you are single, married, divorced, or widowed, you are wanted by your Redeemer! I want us to be women who declare, "I know that my redeemer lives" (Job 19:25).

And because we are redeemed, we have an opportunity to create a legacy of redemption in the lives of others.

Legacy Matters

The Bible is full of genealogies—family trees—that chronicle the origins of our ancestors in the faith. We could easily skip over those long lists and treat them like an outdated Hebrew phone book, full of names that bear no relevance to us. But I don't want us to miss the power and importance of understanding *why* history matters.

When we discuss legacy, we must understand that it is more than the Webster's Dictionary definition: an amount of money or property left to someone in a will, inheritance, or property. The idea of biblical legacy includes our contribution to the next generation. The art you create, the children you raise, the business you build, the scientific contribution you make, the classrooms you impact, the financial freedom you commit to, the music you compose . . . this will be your legacy, and it will impact future generations.

With every step closer to your purpose, with every sacrifice endured, with every promise from God that you hold on to, with every trial you survive, you are adding to the foundation of faith for the next generation to stand upon. The ripple effect of your legacy will reach future generations, for good or for bad, whether we want it to or not. You are creating a legacy one way or another, so the question is, *What will your legacy be?*

Ruth thought of others, honored those around her, and showed up to work. Not only did it give her a sense of purpose, it changed the course of history. Legacy doesn't have to mean leaving a mansion and trust fund behind for a child. Legacy can be as simple and as world-changing as gracefully loving others and honoring those around us. We can find purpose in ordinary acts of everyday life. And when those acts are placed in the hands of an extraordinary God, we will leave some beautiful legacies in our wake.

Asaph, the author of Psalm 78, also knew this and reminded us in verse 4 to declare to the next generation the faithfulness of God: "We will not hide them from their children, but tell to the coming generation the glorious deeds of the LORD, and his might, and the wonders that he has done" (ESV). Legacy is shouting Psalm 145:4 to a deafened world and believing it is true: "One generation shall commend your works to another, and shall declare your mighty acts" (ESV).

Often, we don't realize the weight of our decisions. We think our choices are isolated and independent. But they are so much more.

Ruth was transformed from an idolater to a worshiper, from a widow to a wife, from flat broke to richly blessed. Ruth ran to God in faith, and He blessed her not only with a husband, but also with a son. The baby was named Obed, which means "servant of God," and he went on to be the father of Jesse. And Jesse was the father of David . . . as in KING DAVID. And who came from the lineage of King David? Jesus of Nazareth, who was born in Bethlehem just like his great-great-great-great-great-great (plus another four hundred years of greats) grandfather, Obed.

Imagine if Naomi hadn't wisely advised Ruth to seek out Boaz. Imagine if Ruth had lacked the boldness to approach him. Imagine if Boaz wasn't a man of action and never redeemed Ruth. Where would we be today without the legacy-making moves of our three heroes? Their choices brought gains in each of their lives, for certain. But much more importantly, those same choices became crucial in creating the genealogy that stems from Obed all the way to each of us through the life of Jesus Christ. Do you hear me?! Our girl Ruth is IN THE LINEAGE OF JESUS CHRIST!

Matthew 1 is an unusual ancestral account that includes several very interesting women. Tamar is mentioned in Jesus's family tree, and she solicited sex from her father-in-law and bore Perez. Rahab, who rescued Hebrew spies, was, in fact, a prostitute. Bathsheba gave birth to a son sired by King David out of wedlock. But my favorite woman listed in Jesus's genealogy is none other than our girl Ruth.

Christ our Redeemer came into human history through a totally messed-up family. And if the Son of God had prostitutes and liars and adulterers and murderers in his bloodline, there's hope for you and me, too.

Mildred Rodriguez is living proof.

Redemption Song

Alone and scared, Mildred drove home silently from the clinic. She was reeling with shame and sadness over the decisions she had made. Desperate and alone, she called her friend Laura and told her the painful truth.

Laura got in her car and went straight to Mildred, intentional about being present in her dear friend's pain. She boldly spoke about the redemption of Jesus and how God loved her so much that He could restore her and redeem the pain in her life. He could give her purpose and right all her wrongs.

With three words, Laura forever changed her friend's life: "Jesus loves you."

The love of God pierced Mildred's heart, and that night she made a choice to walk with God as her Savior and friend. Mildred was bold in her decision to give her life to Christ, but the bigger challenge of faith was believing God could take her pain and shame and use it for good.

Moved by the love of Jesus and the changes occurring in her life, Mildred reached out to her ex-boyfriend and invited him to church with her. She wanted him to experience the love and forgiveness she had felt, but he remained cold and callous even months after their breakup.

In a surprise to Mildred and everyone who knew him, her ex eventually accepted an invite to church and asked God to forgive him for his mistakes. He asked Jesus to take full rein over his life and began a new and improved friendship with Mildred. It wasn't long before they were dating again, and then married— both forgiven and reborn children of God.

Mildred and her new husband mourned the decision to terminate their first pregnancy. Through prayers and tears, they asked God to restore and redeem that choice. Mildred prayed, "God, please give me back in grace what I gave up in foolishness."

Within a few months, the newlyweds found out they were pregnant, and their joy was doubled when their first sonogram revealed Mildred was having TWINS. The happy couple burst into tears. God was redeeming their story and their pain for good. The twins would be proof that God not only forgives but redeems.

I'm living proof.

Mildred Rodriguez and her ex-boyfriend-turned-husband, Pancho Juárez, are my parents. The day my twin sister and I came into the world, they wept and thanked God for giving them a double portion of redemption.

When I look at my family—full of immigrants, divorces, abuse, abortion, alcoholism, and so much more—I'm filled with hope. Why? Because there is redemption for all of us. Our redemption will create a legacy, and our legacy will change the future.

Lessons on Legacy

The person you are and the choices you make will not only affect your life but the lives of those in generations to come. When we are redeemed and see what God has done for us, we, too, get to play a role in redeeming others. So let's pull out some practical principles from Ruth and learn how to make sure the legacy we leave is a *good* one.

1. Decisions we make *today* affect our *tomorrow*.

I know I've said this before, but I can't stress it enough. Ruth decided to leave the only land she'd known and travel to a foreign place populated by foreign people. Ruth decided to stay with her mother-in-law when everyone else had left her. Ruth decided to go to work and accept hard, manual labor.

It's important to take stock of our decisions because when we acknowledge the choices we've made, we cannot be victims of circumstance. If we chose our jobs, if we chose our spouses, if we chose our colleges, if we chose our churches, if we chose our cars, we must recognize those are decisions we made. We chose them. We need to own them. We must acknowledge our choices because when life gets hard and situations are messy, we are prone to blame circumstances (or others) for all the things we didn't choose. Though none of us has omnipotent control, this posture is unhealthy.

Ruth did not choose for her husband to die, but she did choose her response to his death. We will all face circumstances out of our control: loss of job, loss of home, loss of health, loss of love—but we all have the ability to choose our responses.

2. *Small* changes make *big* impact.

In the grand scheme of life, we are prone to overlook the small changes that will lead to big changes. Moab was roughly thirty miles away from Bethlehem, but that small journey led Ruth to a life she would've never imagined.

We must constantly be aware of and checking in on the seemingly small changes we make—both for the good and the bad. It is easy to feel overwhelmed by a broad goal like "get in shape" or "give sacrificially." But if you know you need to incorporate exercise into your health routine, the reality is, working out even *once* a week for forty-five minutes will lead to almost SIXTY HOURS of workouts for the year. If you know you should be tithing to your local church, but ten percent feels like too much of a jump, start with one percent. The hardest part of changing is starting. Start with a small change, knowing it can grow into bigger changes.

When my parents had my twin sister and me, they knew a small change would have a big impact on their (eventually five) children. They declared they were going to be a family who attended church regularly. Not a big deal, right? Well, this small decision was the impetus for so many bigger decisions. From my dad walking away from a lucrative (but morally compromising) job, to my mom becoming a principal for a regional homeschooling group, to my dad stepping into the call of ministry on his life, to all five of their children having a love and respect for the community of God, their small decision led to big dividends.

But small changes aren't always good. Be aware of the *unchecked* small changes that could pull you off course. For example, a plane traveling from Los Angeles en route to Washington, DC will end up in Baltimore, Maryland just by being *one degree* off course. What does one degree look like in your life? That relationship you're in just because you're lonely is pulling you off course. The job that is requiring you to compromise your morals is pulling you off course. The multiple glasses of wine that have slipped into your daily routine are pulling you off course. The friend that is so much fun but doesn't positively edify your life is pulling you off course. Not all small things are created equal.

Showing up and being faithful with the *right* small things might just position you for bigger ones! Ruth showed up for the "small" job of working in the field every day and ended the barley harvest season with bags and bags of barley. Plus, she went ahead and bagged Boaz to boot! Amen!

3. Embrace the pain.

Though not expressly stated, Ruth must have dealt with a lot of pain, and she handled it like a champion. Ruth had lost home and husband and still fought to find a way through. During what was undoubtedly a time of hurt, frustration, and confusion, she kept forging forward.

We all experience loss, pain, and death throughout our lives. But redeeming the pain in order to leave a strong legacy will require us to get up after we fall. King Solomon articulated this concept so well when he said, "For though the righteous fall seven times, they rise again" (Proverbs 24:16). We will fall, fail, and falter, not because we suck, but because sometimes life does. We must always find ways to stand back up. According to leadership expert Sam Chand, "Begin to see pain as a great teacher. The more pain you can endure, the more growth you will experience." Don't let pain take you out. There is still more in you.

I'm forever indebted to my mother persistently sharing God's love with her ex-boyfriend after their breakup. Even after he repeatedly rejected her invitation to church—and even after he threw a Bible at her, which she'd given him as a gift—she kept inviting and loving and getting back up. It was undoubtedly the grace of God that brought my father to salvation, but it was my mother's persistence in the midst of pain that wooed my father into a loving relationship with God.

4. Share your story.

The authorship of the book of Ruth is unknown, but most scholars attribute it to the Old Testament prophet Samuel. I'm so grateful for Sam—or whoever wrote the book—because his account helps Ruth's legacy to continue. Her legacy continues not only because of her descendants, but because of her story. Your story needs to be heard. Your story could be the key that unlocks someone else's prison. Has God helped you overcome an eating disorder? Has your faith guided you out of an abusive relationship? Has God healed you of a daunting illness? Don't be afraid to share it.

In the same way that Ruth's story has taught me about resilience and faith, my mother's story has taught many about post-abortion pain and the redemption of God to right all wrongs in His perfect timing. For years, my mother lived in silence and shame, afraid of how others would judge her for her decision to have an abortion. But once she began to step into her story and owned the painful truth, she saw so many women find healing in their own stories. As Brené Brown says in *The Gifts of Imperfection*, "You either walk inside your story and own it, or you stand outside of your story and hustle for your worthiness."[1]

Sometimes God redeems stories by surrounding us with people who need to hear about our pasts in order to help protect their futures. Other times it's simply necessary to display our heartache so someone else can have hope. In all times, we should share our stories, whether utterly ugly or perfectly polished. We share our stories so they can be redeemed and added to our legacies—just like Ruth's.

Boaz didn't know he would redeem a pagan girl from Moab. Ruth didn't know she would birth the grandfather of the greatest king of Israel. Naomi didn't know she would raise a child to whom she had no blood connection yet would love unconditionally. But this is everyday life for people with everyday struggles waiting for everyday miracles. Ruth knew there was no quick-fix solution to make her life not suck. She woke up every morning and went to work.

There is no person, plan, or pill that will instantaneously make your life not suck, either. But if you're willing to do the work, be honest in self-evaluation, and allow yourself to change, you, my darling, are well on your way. But it isn't just about you. Generations to come are depending on you to rise up and lead the way.

Part of the problem with our postmodern mood is a fascination with the *present* and with the question, *What's in it for me?* When we make decisions about our futures, we must remember, our futures will be different—dare I say, more purposeful?—when we think of others before ourselves. We find a new sense of purpose when we give our lives away. Queen Esther knew this when she said, as she risked her life to save her people, "And if I perish, I perish" (Esther 4:16). Paul knew this as he was stoned outside the city walls of Lystra and left to die. Jesus knew this as He hung on the cross for the sins of humanity. In the face of trial, trauma, and tribulation, their purposes were proven when they gave their lives away. How do we know this? Because Queen Esther saved her people from genocide, the apostle Paul—though perceived dead—got back up and continued preaching the gospel, and Jesus rose from the grave as the final victor over death and sin.

Just as my parents accepted Jesus as their personal Lord and Redeemer, you, too, can have a life-transforming encounter with God, who can redeem all the sin, sadness, shame, and sorrow for our good and His glory. I cannot guarantee that you will not have moments of suckiness; in fact, I can pretty much guarantee that you will. But I can also promise that God can redeem even the most painful parts of your story. And once we get a glimpse of what God can do with the broken pieces of our lives, our responses should include telling those around us that our God wants to use *us* to demonstrate what freedom, transformation, and redemption look like.

Don't believe the lie that you can't be used. There is a Savior who sees you wherever you are and wants to use you. It's all right there in Ruth's story, which shows us:

God uses pagans . . .
God uses immigrants . . .
God uses outsiders . . .
God uses widows . . .
God uses the bitter . . .
God uses the hopeless . . .
God uses the suffering . . .
God uses the laborers . . .
God uses the rich . . .
God uses the poor . . .
God uses the young . . .
God uses the old . . .
God uses men . . .
God uses women . . .
God is using me . . .
And God will use you . . .

If your story is not redeemed, your story is not finished.

While this book ends here, your story continues. Write that story every day as a letter to future generations. For the students you teach, for the songs you will write, for the children you might have, for the coworkers who need your hope, for the orphans whose homes you'll build, for the churches that will rise from your generosity, for the redemption you will play in someone's story, keep writing your legacy.

WITH MUCH THANKS

The impossibility of adequately thanking everyone makes me feel as inept as a one-legged man in a butt-kicking contest. But never to be outdone by a challenge, I will begin by thanking the single most influential, probing, prodding, and productive person I know. Matthew Ray Olthoff, I adore you. This book—heck, our entire marriage—would not be what it is without your undying support. You challenge me daily to be the woman you believe I'm destined to be. If you ever try to leave me, I will kill you. Kidding! (Half kidding.)

Melanie Nyema Rozenblatt, you, my dear friend, have the amazing ability to take words and make them come to life. Your honesty, candor, and dedication to this project made this book infinitesimally better. Thank you for saying yes, not just to being my editor, but to fighting for me to be a better communicator.

To the ever-wise Dr. Deborah Gorton, thank you for making hard conversations easier to digest. Your wisdom and insight will change lives, and I'm honored to call you not only my counselor but also my friend.

Mi familia—Mum, Papi, Jazzy, Chu, Alec, Mart, Sagey, Seb, Zobo, Parks, and Ryry—thank you for loving me and allowing me to be crazy, EXTRA, and emotional even when it annoys you. You could leave me, but I'M COMING WITH YOU!

To my homies and forever friends: Bomb Squad (Jasmine,

Brianna, Melanie, and Jennie), I am who I am because of you. The grace you have shown me has marked me forever. Thanks for being my pearls! Lindsey and Alli, since day one you have been my advocates and deepest supporters. Thank you for believing in me when I didn't believe in myself. Roc Queen, you are wise, and I'm truly grateful for all your love and support. Chelsie, we've come a long way, ma! You give me hope for the next generation, and I'm honored to call you SisterFriend. Callie, you demonstrate loyalty and character in everything you do. Thank you for doing life with me (and for watching the world's worst reality television shows and debriefing them like political commentaries). Jeanette and Diane, you are my safe place. No matter what happens, I know we have each other's backs FOR LIFE. For my online social media fam, I'm honored by your engagement, comments, and love. This book is for US. (And mad love to my manicurist Jolene Le for reminding me that life does not suck when you have a good manicure!)

To the church I call home and the baby I get to call mine— The Father's House Orange County—you have made Matt and I parents again, and we are honored to give our lives away for you. Home is the prize, and no matter where we travel, you will always be the place we come running back to.

To our church fam at TFH and Pastor Dave Patterson, thanks for claiming us as your own. HUGE props to Christine Caine for being my Monday Morning Cheerleader and Hope Dealer—you give me faith when I feel like I'm failing. To our dear friends Justin and Stef Dailey, Daniel and Tammie Floyd, Micahn and April Carter, and ARC (shout out to Pastor Dino Rizzo!), we would've failed so many more times if it were not for you. You are forever friends, and Matt and I are LUCKY to call you family.

Shout out to all the amazing people at Zondervan who made this book a reality—David Morris, Carolyn McCready, Bridgette Brooks, Margot Starbuck, Harmony Harkema, and my agent,

Bryan Norman—thank you! Your patience and grace in this process has made this dream become a reality.

Lastly, I want to thank Jesus—my great and glorious Boaz—for being my Redeemer. Life cannot suck because Jesus loves me. Because of His love, I will give my life away and forever tell others how God took me—a crazy Los Angeles Moabitess and immigrant—to be someone who births promises out of barren places and reminds the world that history does not determine our destiny.

NOTES

Chapter 1: Acceptable Stalking

1. L. Lin, et al. "Association Between Social Media Use and Depression Among U.S. Young Adults" *Depression and Anxiety* 33 (April 2016), 323–31.

Chapter 4: Find a Man Who Loves to Give Gifts

1. Quoted in Tara Parker-Pope, "A Gift That Gives Right Back? The Giving Itself," *New York Times*, December 11, 2011, https://www.nytimes.com/2007/12/11/health/11well.html.

Chapter 6: Boaz Over Brokeazz

1. See 1 Samuel 9:1, 1 Kings 11:28, 2 Kings 5:1.
2. Charles Spurgeon, *Works of Charles Spurgeon, Prince of Preachers* (Seltzer Digital Books, 2018), 82.
3. Judges 4–5.
4. Esther 4.
5. 2 Chronicles 34:14–33.

Chapter 7: Say What You Want and Mean What You Say

1. John Gray, *Men Are from Mars, Women Are from Venus: A Practical Guide for Improving Communication and Getting What You Want in Your Relationships* (New York: HarperCollins, 1992).

Chapter 9: Happenstance, Coincidence, or Providence

1. Paraphrased from Walter A. Elwell, ed., *Evangelical Dictionary of Theology*, 2nd ed. (Grand Rapids, MI: Baker Academic, 2001).
2. James 1:17.

Chapter 10: The Inside Outsider

1. Alan Fogel, "Emotional and Physical Pain Activate Similar Brain Regions," *Psychology Today*, April 19, 2012, http://www.psychologytoday.com/us/blog/body-sense/201204/emotional-and-physical-pain-activate-similar-brain-regions.

2. R. F. Baumeister and M. R. Leary, "The Need to Belong: Desire for Interpersonal Attachments as a Fundamental Human Motivation," *Psychological Bulletin* 117 no. 3 (May 1995): 497–529.

3. Amy C. Edmondson and Zhike Lei, "Psychological Safety: The History, Renaissance, and Future of an Interpersonal Construct," *Annual Review of Organizational Psychology and Organizational Behavior* 1 (2014): 23-43.

Chapter 11: Know What You Want

1. Luke 22:42.

Chapter 12: Depressed, Stressed, and Bitter

1. "Mental Illness," National Institute of Mental Health, updated February 2019, https://www.nimh.nih.gov/health-statistics-mental:illness.shtml.

2. "Investing in Mental Health," World Health Organization (2003), http://www.who.int/mental_health/media/investing_mnh.pdf.

3. Romans 12:9.

4. If you can't find your Naomi community in the church, would you be willing to try courage in finding a therapist who holds the same Christian values?

5. M. A. Musick and J. Wilson, "Volunteering and Depression: The Role of Psychological and Social Resources in Different Age Groups," *Social Science and Medicine* 56 no. 2 (January 2003): 259–69.

6. Ruth 4:14–15.

7. Ruth 2:2.

8. Isaiah 53:3–5.

9. Bob Smietana, "Mental Illness Remains Taboo Topic for Many Pastors," LifeWay Research, September 22, 2014, https://lifewayresearch.com/2014/09/22/mental-illness-remains-taboo-topic-for-many-pastors/.

Chapter 14: Sanctified Affliction

1. John 16:33.
2. You can read the full book here: http://www.onthewing.org/user/ Flavel%20-%20Mystery%20of%20Providence%20-%20Modern.pdf.
3. 1 Corinthians 13:12.

Chapter 16: Goodbye Childhood, Hello Womanhood

1. 1 Corinthians 13:11 NASB.

Chapter 18: Be a Strong Woman

1. Melinda French Gates, "Remarks," Powerful Voices Annual Luncheon, October 16, 2003, https://www.gatesfoundation.org/ media-center/speeches/2003/10/melinda-french-gates-2003 -powerful-voices-luncheon.

Chapter 19: Sharing Is Caring

1. Jonathan Meer, David H. Miller, and Elisa Wulfsberg, "The Great Recession and Charitable Giving," NBER Working Paper No. 22902, National Bureau of Economic Research, December 2016, http://www.nber.org/papers/w22902.
2. Elizabeth W. Dunn, Lara B. Aknin, and Michael I. Norton, "Spending Money on Others Promotes Happiness," *Science* 319 no. 5870 (March 21, 2008): 1687–88, http://science.sciencemag.org/ content/319/5870/1687.full.
3. Acts 20:35.

Chapter 21: Do the Hard Work

1. Malcolm Gladwell, *Outliers* (Boston: Little, Brown, 2008), 103.
2. Ibid.

Chapter 22: This Is Just a Season

1. Jeffrey Jensen Arnett, *Emerging Adulthood: The Winding Road from the Late Teens through the Twenties* (New York: Oxford University Press, 2004), 96.
2. Jonathan Vespa, "A Third of Young Adults Live with Their Parents: Jobs, Marriage and Kids Come Later in Life," United States Census Bureau, August 9, 2017, https://www.census.gov/library/ stories/2017/08/young-adults.html.
3. Arnett, *Emerging Adulthood*, 96.

Chapter 23: Werk, Werk, Werk

1. Visit http://www.monitoringthefuture.org for more information.
2. See https://www.convert-me.com/en/convert/history_volume/ bibephah.html?u=bibephah&v=1.

Chapter 24: Redemption and Legacy

1. Brené Brown, *The Gifts of Imperfection* (Center City, MN: Hazelden Publishing, 2010).

Play with Fire

Discovering Fierce Faith, Unquenchable Passion, and a Life-Giving God

Bianca Juaréz Olthoff

Play with Fire, the debut book by popular speaker and teacher Bianca Juaréz Olthoff, is the reminder that God isn't waiting until you have more resources or a spouse or a job so he can use you. He's ready to use you now.

Using the mythical creature, the Phoenix, which was also referenced by early church leaders, she parallels this story with God's work in her own life, highlighting the beauty of reinvention with fire as both the impetus and the method for change. Olthoff reminds us that we serve a God who is redemptive and can take the worst situations and use them for His glory.

Play with Fire is a bible-infused message that will help women discover:

- The way out of the middle is moving forward
- The personal and powerful nature of the Holy Spirit
- The power and sacrifice of transformation
- The unique calling and purpose of life involves transformation

With Olthoff's distinct style, strong storytelling gifts, and powerful bible teaching, *Play with Fire* will remind readers that God has huge dreams for them. In Bianca's words, "He's whispering in the wind and speaking through the fire and shouting in silence the extraordinary dream He is birthing in you. His dream for you is far greater than the dream you have for yourself. It's not your identity or income or influence that will make this happen. Like Zechariah 4:6 says, "'It's not by might nor by power, but by my Spirit,' says the Lord." It's time to play with fire.

Available in stores and online!

ZONDERVAN®
.com